McCUBBIN FAMILY HISTORY

Scottish Gentry, Colonial Founders, and
American Homesteaders

McCUBBIN FAMILY HISTORY

Scottish Gentry, Colonial Founders, and American Homesteaders

Donald G. McCubbin

East of the Mountains and West of the Sun™

RHYOLITE PRESS LLC
Colorado Springs, Colorado

Copyright © 2026 Donald G. McCubbin

All Rights Reserved. No portion of this book may be reproduced in any form or by any electronic or mechanical means, including information storage and retrieval systems, without permission from the publisher, except by a reviewer who may quote brief passages in a review.

Published in the United States of America by
Rhyolite Press, LLC
P.O. Box 60114
Colorado Springs, Colorado 80960
www.rhyolitepress.com

McCUBBIN FAMILY HISTORY
Scottish Gentry, Colonial Founders, and
American Homesteaders

1st edition, January 1, 2026

McCubbin, Donald G.
ISBN: 978-1-943829-76-7
Library of Congress Control Number: Applied for

McCubbin family crest and all maps were hand-drawn by Donald G. McCubbin
Book design and layout: Suzanne Schorsch
Cover design: Don Kallaus

McCubbin

– Prey to None –

Part I	🌿	Scotland
Part II	⚬	Colonial America
Part III	🇺🇸	The United States

Table of Contents

Introduction   xi

Part I: Scottish Gentry

Origins	1
Carrick, the Land and Gentry	5
Tradunnock Farm, Home of the McCubbins	9
Feudal Violence	15
The Kings and the Covenantors	17
Belhamie and Knockdolian	21
Later Owners of Knockdolian	27

Part II: Colonial Founders

Annapolis and Anne Arundel County	31
The First Settlers	35
Brampton, the Home Plantation	39
The Quaker Community of South River	41
John Maccubbin and His Wife or Wives	45
John Maccubbin and His Family	49
Eleanor and Her Second Husband	51
John Maccubbin, Jr., the Eldest Son	55
Richard Maccubbin and Patrick Creagh	59
John Creagh Maccubbin	61
James Maccubbin	62
Zachariah Maccubbin of Brampton	65
Nicholas Maccubbin, Sr. and Mary Clare Carroll	66
Brothers Who Changed Their Surname to Carroll	69
Samuel Maccubbin and Larkin's Hills	71
Moses Maccubbin, the Youngest Son	73
William Maccubbin, Entrepreneur and Soldier	75

Part III: American Homesteaders

Pittsylvania County, Virginia	81
William McCubbin and Eleanor Conley	82
Sons of William McCubbin and the American Revolution	83
Rockingham County, North Carolina	87
Green County, Kentucky	89
James P. McCubbin, Sr. and Family	91
Hancock County, Illinois	99
McCubbin, Bloyd, and Rupe Families	99
Osage River Area, Central Missouri	103
Early Settlers in Osage River Area	104
McCubbins in Benton County, Missouri	106
John McCubbin and the Hawkins/McCubbin Community	108
James P. McCubbin, Jr. and the Hickory Point Community	111
Baptist Church at Hickory Point	112
The Family of James P. McCubbin, Jr.	113
Other Early Families at Hickory Point	116
McCubbins During the Civil War	118
Hickory Point (Watkins) after the Civil War	120
Camden County, Missouri	123
Early Setters on the Auglaize Creek	123
The McCubbin Farmhouse	125
The Auglaize Church	127
Family of Lewis and Jemimah McCubbin	128
Passover and the Passover School	131
McCubbin Family in Linn Creek	134
James Merrill McCubbin	134
Oklahoma	137
Conclusions	143
Notes	*145*
Bibliography	*167*

Illustrations

1.	Map of Carrick, Scotland	3
2.	Map of Tradunnock Farm	8
3.	Tradunnock Manor House	10
4.	Old Stone Barns at Tradunnock	10
5.	"Tradunnock" on Stone Wall	11
6.	Map of Knockdolian and Belhamie	19
7.	Knockdolian Castle	20
8.	Belhamie Farm	21
9.	1600s Date on Knockdolian Castle	22
10	Church at Colmonell	23
11.	Knockdolian Mausoleum	24
12.	McCubbin Coat of Arms	24
13.	Knockdolian House	28
14.	River Stinchar at Knockdolian	28
15.	The "Maryland Dove"	34
16.	Plantation Owner's House	37
17.	Map of Annapolis, Anne Arundel Area	38
18.	Brampton House	55
19.	South River Club	57
20.	Map of Historic Annapolis	58
21.	McCubbin-Patterson House	59
22	The Carroll House	67
23.	Mount Clare Mansion	69
24.	Portrait of James (Maccubbin) Carroll	71
25.	All Hallows Church, South River	72
26.	Map of Virginia/North Carolina Border Area	82
27.	"Wilderness Road" Into Kentucky	91
28.	Map of Eve Area, Green County, Kentucky	92
29.	Vance-McCubbin Cemetery	97
30.	Map of Homesteads, Hancock County, Illinois	98
31.	Map of Osage River Area, Missouri	103
32.	Map of Hickory Point Area, Miller County	108
33.	Hickory Point Church	113
34.	Old Farm Buildings at Hickory Point	121

35.	Map Showing Homesteads in Auglaize Area	124
36.	McCubbin Homestead, Auglaize Creek, Camden County	124
37.	McCubbin Cabin and Farmhouse	126
38.	Lewis and Jemimah McCubbin	126
39.	Auglaize Cemetery Monument	127
40.	"Standing at a Cliff Near Zebra"	128
41.	Passover Log Schoolhouse	131
42.	Passover Students	132
43.	Passover Baseball Team	132
44.	McCubbin Farmhouse Near Tryon, Oklahoma	138
45.	Bruell McCubbin Family in Tryon	138
46.	The Historic Harmony School	139
47.	M&K Grocery Store, Glencoe	141

Introduction

Scotland, in the 1600s, was emerging from a time of feudal violence and was suffering religious struggles and civil war when John Maccubbin left his home and family in Carrick (now South Ayrshire) at a very young age. John's Maccubbin/McCubbin family was a member of the land-owning gentry and was closely associated with other prominent families, including the Kennedys. John arrived in the English colony of Maryland in 1649 as an indentured servant with a group of English Puritans, who claimed free land in the future town of Annapolis and the County of Anne Arundel. After becoming a "freedman," John acquired his own land, Brampton, became a successful planter or farmer, and established a family that prospered as Annapolis became a port city and the capital of colonial Maryland. Some of John Maccubbin's sons continued to be plantation owners, at Brampton and other lands, while the grandsons and great-grandsons became successful businessmen and married into other founding families, including the Creaghs and the Carrolls.

Although some of the Maccubbins continued to live in the Annapolis area, others left, seeking new land and new opportunities in Baltimore and other areas. After 1755, William McCubbin, one of John Maccubbin's grandsons, moved to new settlements in south-central Virginia, when Scots-Irish and German immigrants were arriving there. Three of William's sons served as militiamen during the American Revolution and, after the war, established their families in Rockingham County, North Carolina. In 1806, one of William's son, James P. McCubbin, Sr. took his family west into Kentucky and settled on land that he acquired from the state as a military veteran. As James McCubbin, Sr.'s family grew, some of his sons moved to lands opened to settlement in western Illinois and Missouri, under the Homestead Act. In the 1830s, James McCubbin, Jr. and his brother John helped establish new communities in Miller County, Missouri. After the Civil War, when families and communities were deeply divided, one of James's grandsons, Lewis, started a new community in nearby Camden County, Missouri. Then, in 1919, after former Indian Territory (Oklahoma) was opened to settlement, one of Lewis's sons, Bruell, moved his family to Lincoln County, Oklahoma.

Because the Maccubbin/McCubbin families throughout their history were land-owners, church members, and active members of their communities, they left a record of their lives. Many of the records have been compiled by genealogists in the form of family trees, other genealogical reports, and some published articles. In this writing I have compiled a narrative history of the Maccubbin/McCubbin family in Scotland, of three generations in Maryland, and of one line of those McCubbins as homesteaders in Kentucky, Missouri, and beyond. This history also includes some of the families with whom they intermarried and partnered, including the Kennedys in Scotland, the Howards, Creaghs, and Carrolls in Maryland, and the Lanes, Bloyds, DeGraffenreids, Bartons, and others, with whom they partnered as homesteaders.

The history of the McCubbins and associated families is a testament to the struggles, triumphs, and enduring spirit shared with countless other families who played an important role in the settlement of what would become the United States of America.

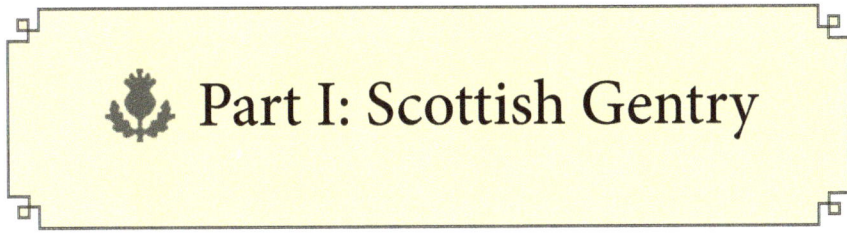

Origins

The very early origin of the Maccubbin/McCubbin family is recorded in their genes. Genetic genealogy (DNA analysis) of American descendants of John Maccubbin tells us that these McCubbins are descended from the ancient Celts who arrived in the British Isles several thousand years ago as farmers and who largely replaced the native hunter-gatherers there.[1] These immigrants spoke a Celtic language called Q-Celtic by linguists, but by about 700 or 800 B.C. the Celts in England, Wales and most of Scotland had begun to adopt a language similar to Welsh or P-Celtic. These Welsh-speaking Celts were never completely subjugated by the Roman armies or by the later Anglo-Saxons and retained much of their language and culture, especially in Wales, northern and western Scotland, and Ireland.[2]

In southwest Scotland (where the earliest MacCubbins/McCubbins are recorded), the Anglo-Saxons arrived in about 700 A.D. but seemingly had little effect on the culture of the indigenous Celtic people there, the Britons.[3] Beginning in about 900 A.D., the Gaelic people began arriving in southwest Scotland from the north of Ireland and the isles of western Scotland. These Gaels were descendants of the Vikings who had intermarried with the native Gaels and had assimilated much of their culture, including the Gaelic language. They were called the Gall-Gaidheal ("stranger Gaels" in Gaelic) and gave name to ancient Galloway, which included much of southwest Scotland.[4]

The name "MacCubbin" may have originated in Galloway after about 1000 AD, when people began assuming surnames that commonly were based on the given name of the father. "MacCubbin" appears to be a Gaelic name because of the prefix "Mac", which is Gaelic for "son of." The

MacCubbins may be of Gaelic origin or, perhaps more likely, they may have been ethnic Britons who adopted a Gaelic name because Gaelic was the dominant language and culture at the time surnames were adopted there.

The earliest record of the name "MacCubbin" was in 1376 in Dumfriesshire and in 1404 in Carrick, when official records were being kept.[5] By this time, the area had come under increasing control by the king of Scotland, and Anglo-Norman systems of law and justice and an early form of English called Old Scots increasingly replaced the Gaelic language and culture.[6] Many of the old Gaelic families, including the Kennedys, continued to resist control by the kings of Scotland but accepted the use of the feudal system of land ownership. After the Protestant Reformation in 1560, the resistance against the king came to involve religious and as well as legal and political differences.

John Maccubbin, immigrant, was born in about 1632, as estimated from the time of his arrival in Maryland and the time of his death. It is believed, from the study of the DNA of John's American descendants and the circumstances of time and place, that John Maccubbin was the son of Fergus McCubbin and Margaret Kennedy, who owned the lands of Tradunnock and, later, Knockdolian in Carrick, southwest Scotland.[7]

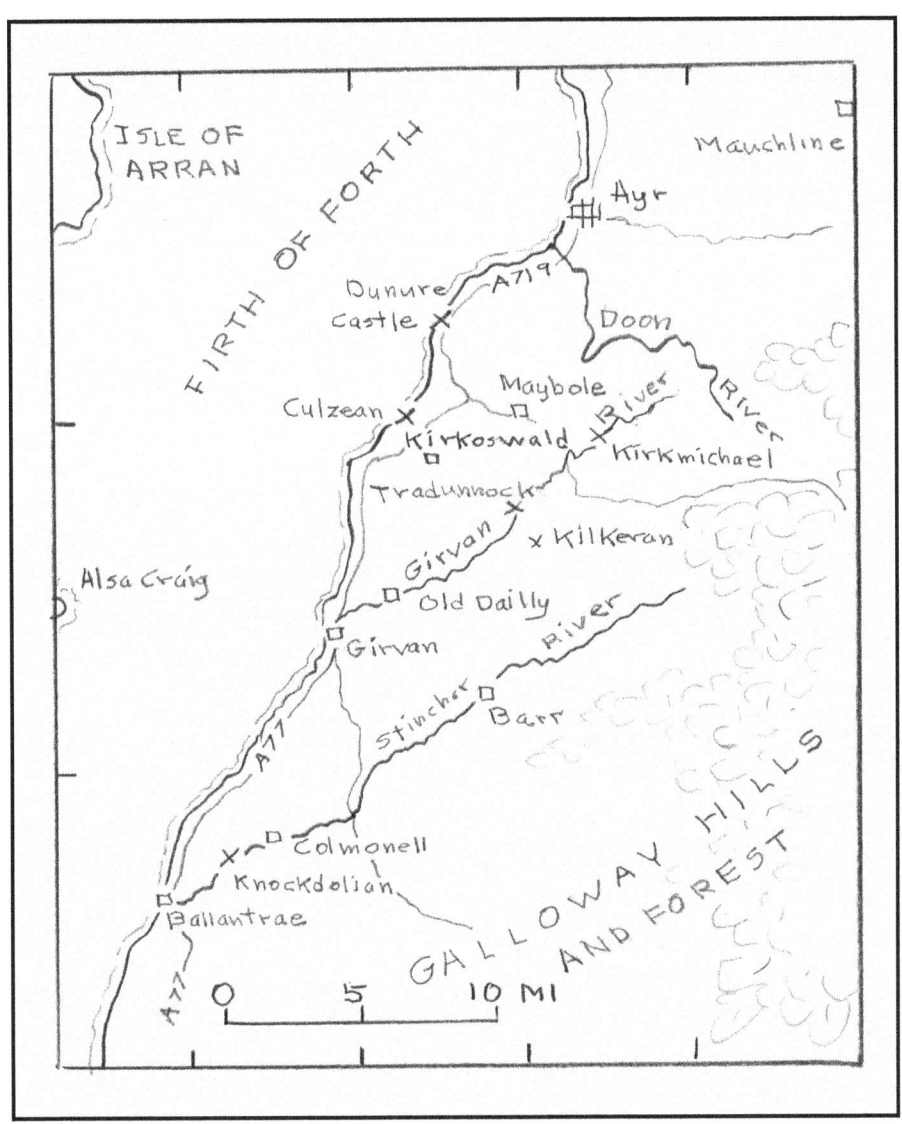

Carrick, southwest Scotland, is bordered on the south and southeast by the Galloway Hills, on the west by the Firth of Forth (an arm of the Irish Sea), and on the north by the River Doon. Maybole, the ancient capital of Carrick, and Girvan are the largest towns. Tradunnock, on the Girvan River, and Knockdolian, on the River Stinchar, are farms formerly owned by the McCubbins of Carrick.

Carrick, the Land and Gentry

Carrick, formerly part of old Galloway, is now a district in Ayrshire and includes most of the area that is called South Ayrshire. Carrick is a small, sparsely populated land, bordered on the south and southeast by Dumfries & Galloway, on the west by the Firth of Clyde (an arm of the Irish Sea), and on the north by the River Doon. It is a land of wooded hills and grassy plains, watered by three clear, rushing rivers, the Doon, the Girvan, and the Stinchar, which originate in the Galloway Hills and Forest. The town of Maybole was the ancient capital of Carrick, and Ayr, just across the border in North Ayrshire, was the largest town in the area. Ayr, the capital of Ayrshire, became a royal burgh in 1203, and Maybole become a burgh in 1516. Girvan, on the main highway through Carrick, was originally a small seaport and now is the commercial center of Carrick. Other towns in Carrick include the historic parish villages, Kirkoswald, Maybole, Kirkmichael, Girvan, Dailly, Barr, Ballantrae, Colmonell, and Stratton. The main highway through Carrick extends along the coast to Ayr, the county seat of Ayrshire, and beyond to the metropolis of Glasgow.

Historically, Carrick is a land of farmers and herders, famous for its sheep and cattle. Its earliest industry was that of the craftsmen and weavers who made the yarns and textiles.[8] The Reverend William Abercrummie, minister of the church in Maybole, wrote in 1696 that Carrick "is better fitted for pasturage than Corns, yet it produces such plenty of all sorts of graine, that it not only serves its own Inhabitants, but has plenty to spare to neighbouring places."[9] More recently, the boggy river valleys have been drained to enhance the pastures, and modern agricultural methods have been introduced by many of the land owners. Some of the farm owners, including the Fergussons, still live on their historic estates.

Until recently, the farms and estates of Carrick were owned and operated under the feudal system—by a "superior" or by his tenant who paid rent to his superior. A superior commonly feued his land to a "vassal," who in turn could feu the land down to anther vassal. Land could be "sold" by resigning it to a superior, who then could reassign it to another new "owner." This could be accomplished by "the giving of sasine," whereby the land owner transferred his land by the symbolic transfer of a handful of rocks and soil to the new owner. Formal "deeds of conveyance" were then recorded in the Charters of the Abbey of Crossraguel and, after 1617, in the Registers of Sasines. Many of the early records, written in Latin or Old Scots, are archived in the National Records of Scotland.

During the time of the McCubbins in Carrick, there were some thirty-five land-owning families whose properties are described by Rev. Abercrummie and by other early historians such as Patterson. These families included the McCubbins, as well as the McAlexanders, Cathcarts, Fergussons, and others, but about half of the land-owning families were branches of the large and diverse Kennedy clan. These branches included the Kennedys Earls of Cassillis and the Kennedys of the house of Bargany They also included the Kennedys of Drummelane and the Kennedys of Kirkmichael, with whom the McCubbins had connections by marriage.[10]

Symson, who wrote in 1660, refers to the power and influence of the Kennedys of Carrick in a rhyme:

> "Twixt Wigton and the toun of Ayr,
> Portpatrick and the Cruives of Cree,
> No man needs think for to bide there,
> Unless he court with Kennedie."[11]

Many members of the land-owning gentry of Carrick, including the Kennedys, had owned their lands for hundreds of years, passing them down according to the traditions of the clan system and male-preferred primogeniture. In contrast, the McCubbins, although they may have been related to landowners in Dumfriesshire, acquired their land at Tradunnock by, first, being tenants and, then, by purchasing the property. As the McCubbins grew their land holdings, they established relationships with neighboring families, including, as mentioned above, two branches of the Kennedy clan, the Kennedys of Drummelane and the Kennedys of Kirkmichael. Like other land owners, the McCubbins passed down their property according to the laws of primogeniture, that is, to the eldest son, or failing that to his eldest son, or failing that to the nearest male member of the family.

The landed gentry were identified in the records by the names of their home estates. An individual who owned a property was identified as "**of**" that estate or property. One who lived in a property but did not own it (as, for example, a tenant) was identified as "**in**" the property. Individual land owners were sometime referred to only by the name of their home property. Thus, for example, Fergus McCubbin, the laird of Knockdolian, was sometimes referred to simply as "Knockdolian."

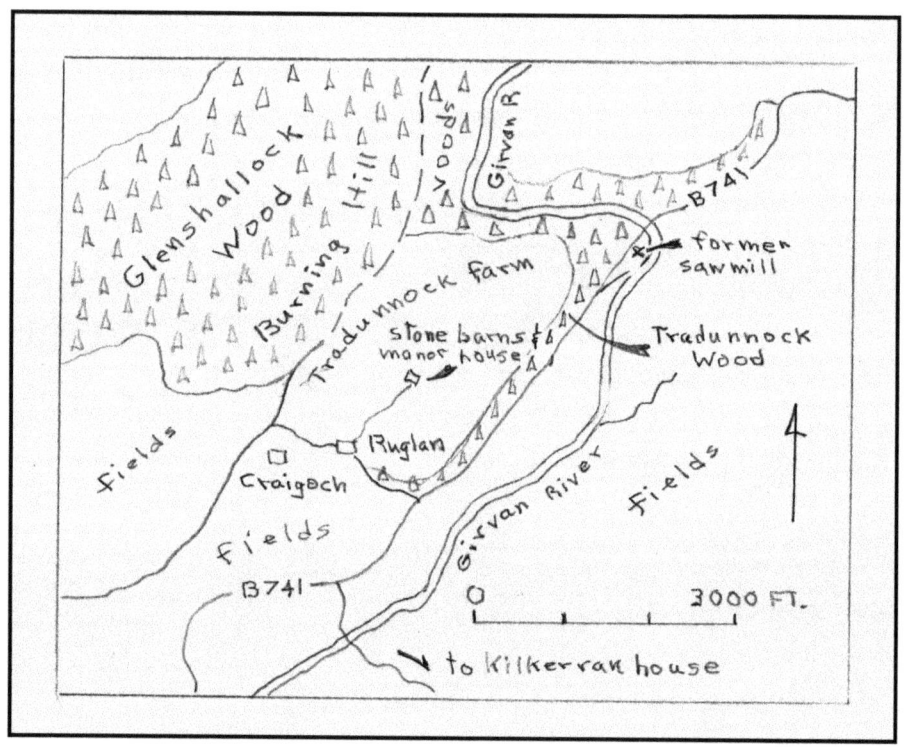

Tradunnock farm, now part of the estate of the Fergussons of Kilkerran, was the home of the McCubbins from 1404 to about 1642. The Tradunnock manor house and three stone barns are located at the end of a driveway northeast of the farm buildings at Ruglan. "Burning Hill,' the site of a former coal mine, and the woods surrounding Tradunnock farm appear in the earliest descriptions of the area.

Tradunnock Farm, Home of the McCubbins

Tradunnock is a farm in the parish of Dailly, only a few miles from Crossraguel Abbey and Maybole, which didn't become a burgh or town until 1516. A map published in 1859 shows that Tradunnock then was much as it is today, with the farm buildings at the entrance to the farm at Ruglan and the main residence house at the end of a long driveway in the middle of the farm. When I visited Tradunnock in August 2007, the handsome house of Tradunnock was occupied by one of the sons of the Fergusson family, the present owners of the property. The only structures near the residence house are three very large stone barns which date before the 1859 map and some ancient stone fences with the name "Tradunnock" carved in the stones. There are no ruined castles on the property, but it is possible that the stone barns were built with the stones from a much older castle or other fortified dwelling. The stones from abandoned structures were reused in this way on many other properties.

The earliest McCubbin at Tradunnock was a John Makcubyn, who was named in the records as a tenant at "Tredonag" (Tradunnock) in 1404, when it was a feudal property owned by the MakAlexander family.[12] In 1492, Dougal MacCuben, probably the son of John, was living at "Tradonnog McCubbing", evidently as a tenant, when it was acquired by Thomas Kennedy of Bargany.[13] In 1511, Thomas McCubbin, probably a son of Dougal, held Tradunnock as a tenant. Then, in 1548, Thomas became full owner when "Thomas Kennedy of Bargany gave sasine with his own hands to Thomas McCubbyn of the 10-schilling lands of Knockbrockloch, alias Trodenat."[14]

The next owner of Tradunnock was Archibald McCubbin, probably

Tradunnock house, now the residence of one of the sons of the Fergusson family, is located near three old stone barns and an ancient stone fence, and overlooks the valley of the Girvan River and Kilkerran house below. It may be near the site of the former McCubbin home at Tradunnock farm. (Photo by the author, August 2007.)

Three large stone barns, one of which is seen here, probably date from the 1800s. These barns, like other stone structures in Carrick, may have been built with the stones from a ruined stone castle on the site. (Photo by the author, August 2007.)

the son of Thomas. Records show that Archibald McCubbin married the daughter of Hew Kennedy of the House of Drummelane. When Archibald died in 1580, he left considerable wealth to his eldest son, another John, who evidently was underage at the time.[15] It was not until 1619 that this John was officially recognized as owner of Tradunnock, when "sasine was given to him."[16] John McCubbin, heir to Tradunnock, had, in 1606, married Jonet Kennedy, daughter of Alexander and Margaret Kennedy of Drummelane.[17] Thus John was the second generation of McCubbins to marry into the Kennedys of Drummelane, an old and prominent family, whose castle was on the headwaters of the Girvan River near Tradunnock.[18] Alexander and Margaret Kennedy left the life-rent of several of their properties to Jonet, who was identified in their wills as "John M'Cubein's wyf."[19]

"Tradunnock" is carved in the stones of an ancient stone fence near the present house and old barns. This fence, which frames the view of the Girvan River Valley and Kilkerran House below to the southwest, may be the oldest relict structure on the farm. (Photo by the author, August 2007.)

When John McCubbin, laird of Tradunnock, died in July 1620, he left to his wife Jonet Kennedy the life-rent of Tradunnock and 300 merks, plus an additional 300 merks yearly "for the upbringing of their children" (who were unnamed and were all underaged at the time).[20] John and Jonet had two children, Fergus and John. Fergus must have been the elder son, but he was not recognized as owner of Tradunnock until 1631, probably when he reached legal age.[21] It was at about the same time (1630-1631) that Fergus married Margaret Kennedy, daughter of Thomas Kennedy of Kirkmichael, the laird of a family whose property was a few miles from Tradunnock on a tributary of the Girvan River.[22] The Kennedys of Kirkmichael, like the Kennedys of Drummelane were an old and prominent family. Both families traced their ancestry to the early chiefs of the Kennedy clan.[23]

After Fergus McCubbin and Margaret Kennedy of Kirkmichael were married in 1630-1631, they continued living at Tradunnock, and this is probably where John Maccubbin and his brothers were born.[24] Fergus and Margaret moved their family to the Colmonell area, farther south in Carrick, sometime before 1642, when records show that Fergus was an Elder or Presbyter of the church at Colmonell. Although they had moved away, Fergus continued to be the owner of Tradunnock, and, by 1643, he was also the owner of the property of Girvanmayns "with the Grain Mill, the Cruives and fishings of the same."[25] Fergus must have been receiving income from these and perhaps other properties.

John Maccubbin the immigrant was born in about 1632, as estimated from the time of his arrival in Maryland as an indentured servant, the date of his marriage, and the time of his death. He almost certainly was a member of the Tradunnock family, and, as mentioned above, he probably was one of the sons of Fergus and Margaret McCubbin of Tradunnock, who were married in 1630-1631. There are no records that prove this origin, perhaps because he was too young to be mentioned in the records before he left home for the colonies, but the Y-DNA of modern descendants of John Maccubbin have an exact or near-exact DNA match with a McCubbin whose family headstone is in Dailly, near Tradunnock, and whose family claims descent from the McCubbins of Knockdolian.[26]

We do not know how long the property of Tradunnock may have stayed in McCubbin hands. Fergus McCubbin was owner of Tradunnock in 1642 when he and Margaret were living at Belhamie. It is possible that Fergus's brother John was living at Tradunnock at the time, but there is no record that he ever became owner. The next known owners of Tradunnock, after the McCubbins, was the Reverend John Burns, minister of the church at Kirkoswald, and his heirs.[27] In 1699, Tradunnock was acquired by the Fergussons of Kilkerran for non-payment of debt, but in 1700 Gilbert Goldie became tenant of the property by marriage to Christian Burns, probably a daughter of the previous occupants.[28] Today, as mentioned before, Tradunnock is still part of the estate of the Fergussons of Kilkerran.

Feudal Violence

One of the ancient branches of the Kennedy family held the title of Earl of Carrick after 1372 and the title of Earl of Cassillis after 1505. In 1526, the Earl of Cassillis became involved in a deadly feud with the Campbells of Loudon, and other members of the Kennedy clan were also involved in this feud in support of the Earl, the chief of their clan.[29] It appears the some of the McCubbins of Tradunnock were also involved, probably in support of some of the Kennedys of Drummelane and Kirkmichael, with whom they were connected as neighbors and by marriage.[30]

Later, after 1570, a feud between two members of the Kennedy clan, the Earl of Cassillis and the Kennedys of Bargany resulted in deadly conflict. This conflict was triggered when the Earl of Cassillis abducted the Commendator of the Abbey of Crossraguel and tortured him in his castle at Dunure in an effort to gain control of certain feudal properties held by the abbey. In response, Gilbert Kennedy of Bargany stormed the castle of the Earl and rescued the Commendator.[31] The "Commendator" was an administrator, appointed by the Crown to manage the assets of the abbey after it effectively was closed following the Protestant Reformation.

This feud became deadly in December 1601, when a large party led by the Earl of Cassillis confronted Gilbert Kennedy of Bargany and a small group of his supporters in armed conflict at Brockloch Burn near Maybole. (This Gilbert was the young son of the Gilbert who had attacked the castle of the Earl). The young Gilbert Kennedy fought bravely in his defense in this conflict, but was mortally wounded by the Earl's men.[32] In retribution, Bargany's brother and other supporters attacked and killed another member of the Kennedy clan, the laird of Culzean, who was a supporter of the Earl.[33] Two of these supporters were arrested and eventually executed on orders of the King.[34] Gilbert Kennedy's wife died in 1605, just four years after the death of her husband. Because her son was only four-years old, their property was placed under the control of a "tutor" or guardian. The property was soon lost to creditors and, by 1640, the ancient House of Bargany was extinquished.[35]

During these events, the McCubbins lived at Tradunnock farm in northern Carrick, near the castles of Cassillis at Dunure and Maybole. Their friends, the Kennedys of Drummelane and Kirkmichael, may have been pressured to take sides in the feud, but there is no evidence that any of the members of these families were involved in the feudal violence. By 1631, when Fergus McCubbin of Tradunnock married Margaret Kennedy of Kirkmichael, the feud and its aftermath had passed into history. John Maccubbin, who was born about 1632, may have heard stories about these events from his family.

The Kings and the Covenantors

Peace in Carrick was disturbed again when the Kings of Scotland tried to impose greater control over the Presbyterian church, which had become the dominant church in Scotland after the Protestant Reformation. King James VI and his successors, Kings Charles I and Charles II, who were kings of both Scotland and England, sought to place the Church of Scotland under the rule of the bishops of the Church of England and the King, who was head of the Church. Resistance led to widespread support for a National Covenant against these changes, and in 1639 and again in 1640 King Charles I went to war against his subjects in Scotland.[36] After the "Covenantors" gained control of the Scottish Parliament, they became involved in the Civil War between Charles I and the English Parliament under Cromwell.

In Carrick, some eighty-seven men, mostly members of the landed gentry, were signers of the National Covenant in 1638.[37] These signers included several families closely associated with the McCubbins of Tradunnock. Although the McCubbins of Tradunnock may not have been signers of the Covenant, they undoubtedly were Presbyterians at the time and may have been sympathetic to the Covenantors. Earlier parish records are lost, but, by 1646, Fergus McCubbin and his father-in-law David Kennedy of Kirkmichael were active members of the Presbyterian church at Colmonell. Also, in 1647, both Fergus and David were participants in a "Committee of War" for the County of Ayr, which evidently was formed to raise men and supplies for an army in support of the Covenantors.[38]

The earliest battle of this civil war that may have involved the people of Carrick was in June 1648 at Mauchline Muir in East Ayrshire, just north of Carrick, when a group of Presbyterians who had gathered there were attacked by Scottish soldiers who supported King Charles I.[39] In August, 1648, a Scottish army supporting King Charles I in his war with Oliver Cromwell and the English Parliament was defeated in the Battle of Preston in Lancashire. In battles in Scotland and England in 1650 and 1651, thousands of Scottish soldiers were killed and captured by English armies.

At the time of the attack on the Presbyterians at Mauchline Moor in 1648, Fergus and Margaret McCubbin were living at Belhamie in southwestern Carrick, and it seems unlikely that they or their friends, the Kirkmichaels, were present at the battle of Mauchline Moor. John Maccubbin may have already left home, arriving in Maryland by way of Virginia in 1649. He had certainly left home by the time of the later battles of this war, when many Scots were sent to the colonies as prisoners of war.[40]

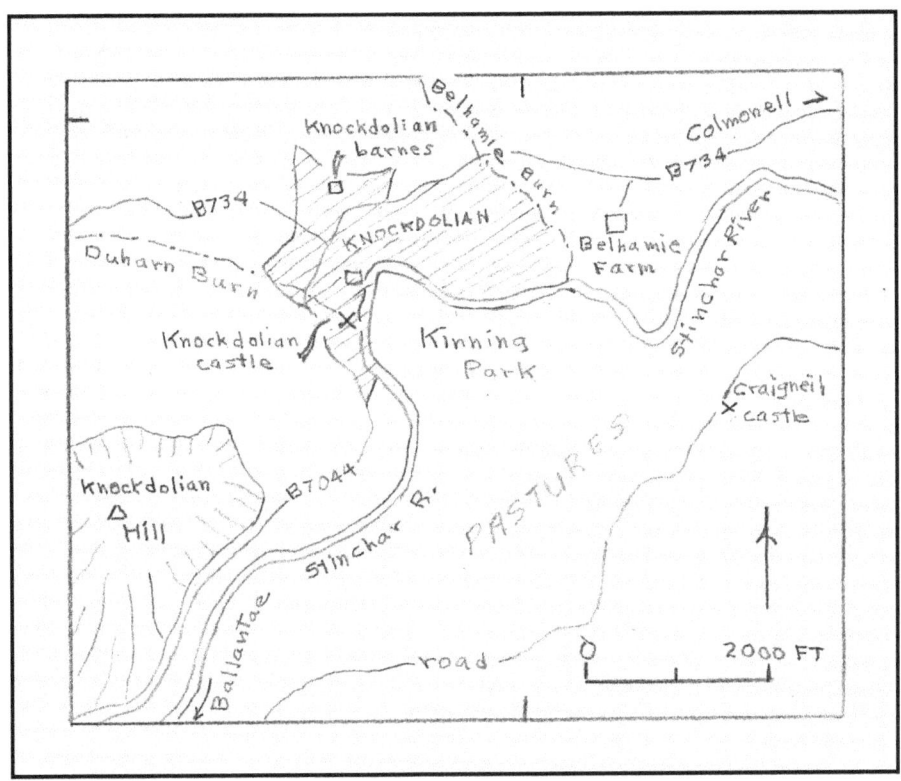

Knockdolian estate and Belhamie farm are located on the northwest side of the River Stinchar and at the base of Knockdolian Hill, one of the most prominent topographic features of the area. The old castle, "home of the McCubbins," and a courtyard in front of the castle are separated by a small burn from the manor house and gardens of Knockdolian estate.

Knockdolian castle, a fortified four-story tower, was built by Fergus and Margaret McCubbin "on the foundation of a much older structure" and was the home of the McCubbin family from about 1653 to 1722. The castle is nearly intact, except for the roof and part of the top attic level. (Photo by the author, August 2007.)

Belhamie and Knockdolian

By 1642, Fergus and Margaret McCubbin had moved from Tradunnock to the farm of Belhamie, near the parish village of Colmonell, in the southwest corner of Carrick. Belhamie may have been owned by David Kennedy of Kirkmichael as part of the nearby estate of Knockdolian. David evidently lived at Knockdolian at the time, because both he and Fergus were elders of the church at Colmonell in 1643. Belhamie and Knockdolian are located on the River Stinchar, between Colmonell and the mouth of the river on the coast at Ballantrae. The Stinchar was described by Robert Burns in his poem *My Nanie, O*: "Beyond yon hills, where Stinchar flows, 'mang moors an' mosses many, O."

Belhamie farm, now part of the Knockdolian estate, was the home of Fergus and Margaret McCubbin after they left Tradunnock. The view here is of the present buildings at Belhamie farm, with Knockdolian Hill in the background. (Photo by the author, August 2007.)

In 1653, after David Kennedy died, Fergus McCubbin in Belhamie purchased Knockdolian and the estate of Glentig from John Kennedy of Kirkmichael, David's son and heir, for 32,000 merks (1600 pounds sterling).[41] Fergus and Margaret must have moved into the ancient castle on the estate of Knockdolian at about this time. (An ancient sundial with the date of 1658 and the initials "F. McC." was found on the grounds there.)[42] John Maccubbin the immigrant may have been living with Fergus and Margaret at Belhamie, but he had certainly left home for the colonies in America by the time Fergus and Margaret moved into Knockdolian.

An engraved shield with the partly illegible date "16??" in a stone above a second-story window shows that the castle was built during the time that Fergus and Margaret McCubbin lived there, in the 1600s. (Photo by the author, August 2007.)

The castle of Knockdolian, much of which still stands today, is a four-story stone tower with a dining hall on the second floor and a laird's suite of two rooms on the third floor. The fourth-floor attic may have been an additional bedroom.[43] The castle is said to have been built on the foundation of a much older structure, but Fergus and Margaret McCubbin built most of the existing castle because the date 16?? (partly illegible date in the 1600s) is carved in the stone above one of the second story windows. The McCubbins also must have had outbuildings in the courtyard and on the riverside nearby. The roof and part of the attic level are missing from the castle, but the structure is otherwise well preserved. The stone remnants of an ancient mill are preserved on the riverside below.

The present Church of St Colmon of Ella in the village of Colmonell was built in 1772, but a plaque on the building that it replaced read "Heir is ane hous built to serve God, 1591," perhaps an indication of when the original church was built. (https://www.colmonell.scot). Minutes of the church show that Fergus McCubbin was an elected Elder between 1644 and 1651, representing the Colmonell church at the Presbytery in Ayr. (Photo by the author, August 2007.)

The estate of Knockdolian was described by the Reverend William Abercrummie in 1696 as "the seat of the McKubbens about which is shewen what art and industrie can do to render a place, to which nature hath not been favorable, very pleasant by planting of gardens, Orchards, walks, and rows of trees, that surprise the beholder with things so far beyond expectation in a country so wild and mountainous."[44] Reverend Abercrummie may have considered the area of Knockdolian to be "wild and mountainous" because it was near the hills and forests that separated Carrick from Galloway to the south and was relatively distant from the more populated areas near Maybole and Ayr in the north of Carrick.

The Knockdolian family mausoleum is the largest burial structure in the churchyard at Colmonell and is intact except for the roof. It was built in 1663 by Fergus and Margaret McCubbin and has served the Knockdolian families since that time. (Photo by the author, August 2007.)

The McCubbin coat of arms, with the hawk on the helmet symbolizing the motto "Prey to None," is on the front of the mausoleum above the door. The coat of arms for Margaret Kennedy McCubbin, with the initials M and K, is on an inside wall opposite the door. (Photo by the author, August 2007.)

Fergus and Margaret McCubbin built the family burial vault in the churchyard of their parish church at the village of Colmonell in 1663. This stone mausoleum, which is complete except for the roof, has the coat of arms of the McCubbins of Knockdolian on the outside above the door and the coat of arms of Fergus's wife, Margaret Kennedy, with the initials M and K, on the inside wall opposite the door. On the McCubbin coat of arms a hawk, perched on the helmet, symbolizes the family motto "Prey to None."[45]

As mentioned earlier, Fergus McCubbin was a church elder of the church at Colmonell by 1642. Although Fergus may not have been a signer of the Covenant in 1638, he and other members of the McCubbin family were active supporters of the Presbyterian church by 1674, when the kings of Scotland were continuing to suppress the Covenantors and their supporters. Those supporters included some Presbyterian ministers who continued to hold illegal services, called "conventicles," in private homes or in the open fields. One of those ministers, Anthony Shaw, was the minister of the church at Colmonell and was the husband of Fergus McCubbin's sister, Agnes. In 1674, Anthony Shaw was arrested and jailed because he "preached at Knockdolian's house in Colmonell [Parish]."[46] This "Knockdolian," of course, was Fergus McCubbin, the laird of the house of Knockdolian.

Fergus McCubbin, Sr., the first McCubbin laird of Knockolian, died in 1677. He and Margaret had two sons, David, who married Agnes Chalmers, and Fergus, Jr., who married Kathrine Montgomery. He also had a brother, John of Balhamie, who died in Antrim, Ireland. David was the eldest son according to the records and would have been the first heir, but he died before his father, so David's son, another Fergus, became the heir to Knockdolian. But this Fergus died at about the same time as his grandfather, Fergus, Sr. As a result, under the rules of primogeniture, Fergus, Jr., surviving son of Fergus, Sr. and nephew of John of Balhamie, became the heir and succeeded to Knockdolian in 1677 when his father died. (This understanding of the ownership of Knockdolian after the death of Fergus, Sr. is based on the analysis of the records by Scottish genealogist Diane Baptie and Lorna McCubbin and is reported on the McCubbin history website.[47]) Note that John Maccubbin might have inherited Knockdolian had he stayed in Carrick, but by 1677 he had been in the colony of Maryland for 28 years and had become a successful planter and family man.

Fergus McCubbin, the second Fergus of Knockdolian, was a strong supporter of Scottish Presbyterianism. He was arrested and imprisoned in 1678 and again in 1683 for "rebellion, reset of rebels and other treasonable crimes," shortly after he had become laird of Knockdolian. In the following year he and a number of others were again before the Privy Council on a similar charge. He was accused of giving sanctuary and support to Alexander Peden, one of the most prominent covenanting ministers in Carrick, and was heavily fined for it.[48] It was at this time, in 1678, that the King sent some 9000 Scottish troops (the "Highland Host") into Ayrshire to arrest the Covenantors who continued to hold their religious meetings in the illegal "conventicles."[49] It was during this period that a large number of Scots arrived in the American colonies, many of them identified as Covenantors.[50]

Later Owners of Knockdolian

The second Fergus, laird of Knockdolian, died in about 1710. He had no sons, and after his death Knockdolian passed into hands of the Cathcarts of Genoch by rights of Fergus's daughter Margaret. Knockdolian then passed to succeeding generations of Cathcarts, and, in March 1840, Alexander Cathcart became owner of Knockdolian. In 1842, this Alexander sold the family estate of Genoch and built a "commodiouse and elegant mansion"[51] at Knockdolian for his new wife. In 1871, the Cathcarts sold the Knockdolian estate to William McConel of Manchester, who lived there with his family until his death in 1902.[52] William McConel's granddaughter, Diana Ruth McConel, inherited Knockdolian and in 1944 married Arthur Valerian Wellesley, the 8th Duke of Wellington.[53] Lady Diana, the Duchess of Windsor, was the owner of Knockdolian when Donald McCubbin visited there in August 2007.

The owners of the Knockdolian estate have protected and preserved the old stone castle of Knockdolian and have continued to be patrons of the church at Colmonell, where the stone mausoleum built by Fergus and Margaret McCubbin is still the largest monument in the churchyard. The spectacular gardens at Knockdolian estate are sometimes open to public view, and members of a local fishing club are allowed to fish for salmon in the River Stinchar at Knockdolian.

The fine gothic mansion, Knockdolian House, was built after about 1842 by Alexander Cathcart, whose family acquired Knockdolian estate in 1722 by marriage to the daughter of the last of the McCubbins to live there. (Photo by the author, August 2007.)

The River Stinchar, viewed here from Knockdolian House, is a clear rushing stream and an active salmon fishery. (Photo by the author, August 2007.)

Part II: Colonial Founders in Maryland

Annapolis and Anne Arundel County

Annapolis and the surrounding area of Anne Arundel County, Maryland, is a low-lying plain, indented by many tidal rivers, on the west side of Chesapeake Bay. The old historic part of Annapolis is a small peninsula bounded on the northeast by College Creek and the Severn River and on the southwest by Spa Creek. When the first settlers arrived in 1649, the area was a watery, unspoiled wilderness. One newcomer sailing up the bay said the shoreline looked "like a forest standing in water."[54] These settlers, probably at least eighty individuals, traveled some 140 miles up Chesapeake Bay from Norfolk, Virginia to this previously unsettled land, which they called New Providence.[55] They had been specifically invited to be the first settlers in the area by Lord Baltimore, proprietor of the colony of Maryland, and were promised one hundred acres of land for each settler, family member, or indentured servant, and complete freedom of religion.[56]

Some of these new settlers claimed land on the future townsite and established boat landings in the natural creeks or coves there.[57] Most, however, took up claims of 50 to 400 acres each in the area to the west and south in Anne Arundel County, where they established new tobacco plantations.[58] Because there were no roads, except pathways made by the Indians, the new town was slow to develop as a trading port. For many years, the plantation owners rolled their heavy hogsheads of tobacco to the waterfront and traded with passing English ship captains. George Alsop, who wrote in 1666, advising a friend about sending a factor (agent) to trade for him in Maryland, told him "That the Factor whom you employ be a man of Brain, otherwise the Planter will go near to make a Skimming dish of his skull."[59]

There is very little written about Annapolis, first called Anne Arundel Town, as it was during the first forty years of its existence, but it must have been a raw little colonial town with only a few houses and other buildings.[60] "The streets were unpaved and unlighted; pigs and cows roamed at will; tanneries rendered the air somewhat less than salubrious."[61] In 1682, the colonial Assembly of Maryland made the town an official port and authorized the surveyor to lay out numbered lots.[62] Later, in 1694, Maryland became a royal colony, and the Assembly moved the provincial capital from St. Mary's to Anne Arundel Town, which in the following year was renamed Annapolis. As a royal colony, the Episcopal (formerly Anglican) Church became the official church of Maryland and St. Anne's, the first church in Annapolis, was built.[63]

In 1707, Annapolis became the official port of entry for the Upper Chesapeake Bay, and ships carrying manufactured articles and luxury goods from England unloaded their merchandise there and returned with tobacco, grain, and other products of the nearby plantations.[64] In the 1740s, the entrepreneur Patrick Creagh contracted to build government buildings, and he also established a shipyard in Annapolis. He was one of the first to operate his own ships in the trade with England.[65] By the 1750s, some of the plantation owners, including members of the Maccubbin family, became successful businessmen and property owners in Annapolis.

Shortly before the beginning of the Revolutionary War, the "Sons of Liberty" met on the campus of St. John's College, and, in 1774, a mob burned the English brig *Peggy Stewart* in protest of the Stamp Act. The colonial government was overthrown in 1775, and the governor of Maryland left Annapolis on a British frigate.[66] Annapolis saw no combat during the war, but citizens of the area, including great-grandsons of John Maccubbin, served in the Maryland militia and in the Continental Army.

In late 1783 and in 1784 the Continental Congress met in the State House in Annapolis, ratified the treaty which brought the Revolutionary War to an end, and accepted the resignation of George Washington as Commander of the Continental Army.[67] At the ball honoring General Washington, Martha Rolle Maccubbin, the 20-year-old wife of James Maccubbin of Annapolis, was chosen by General Washington as his partner, as described in an article in the *New York Times*.[68]

After the Revolution, Baltimore became the main port for Maryland, and Annapolis declined in economic and social influence. Today, Annapolis is still the capital of Maryland, the home of the U. S. Naval Academy, and a suburb of the rapidly-growing Washington D.C. area. The early history of the "ancient city" of Annapolis is preserved in the buildings of the downtown historic district, including the State Assembly building, St. Anne's Church, and some of the early residences.[69] In one of those historic buildings, the governor's mansion, a portrait of Queen Henrietta Maria (for whom Maryland is named), painted by Florence Mackubin, a descendant of John Maccubbin, is hanging in the entry hall.[70]

Historic houses in Annapolis include those owned and occupied by members of the Maccubbin family. One of those, the "Carroll House", built in 1722 by Dr. Charles Carroll, was owned and occupied by members of the Maccubbin family from 1776 to 1799. This house was extensively restored and modernized and moved to the campus of St. John's College.[71] Other historic houses at 110 and 160 Prince George Street, near the original harbor, were owned by the Creagh/Maccubbin family.[72] Many of the historic plantation houses in the area around Annapolis have been designated as historic properties.[73] One of these, Brampton, the plantation house built in about 1740 by a son of John Maccubbin, is still occupied as a residential property in the neighborhood where many of John Maccubbin's Quaker friends lived, and where one of the streets today is called "Friends Road."[74]

The 'Maryland Dove' is a full-sized replica of the English ship that brought the settlers to St. Mary's City, the first settlement in Maryland and now a state historic area. The ships that brought John Maccubbin and other early immigrants to the colonies probably were very similar. (Photo by the author, June 2001.)

The First Settlers

In the fall of 1649, a group of about eighty settlers, mostly English Puritans, arrived in the Annapolis area, where they were promised new land and complete freedom of religion. They left older settlements in Lower Norfolk County, Virginia, where they were threatened with legal action and confiscation of their property for refusing to support the Church of England, the established church of Virginia, an English royal colony.[75] These new settlers took up land grants in the area that would become the town of Annapolis and in nearby parts of Anne Arundel County. Within a few years they had their land surveyed and patented, giving them legal possession. These original patent owners, who had claimed much of the land of the area, became the founding families of Anne Arundel County and Annapolis.[76]

One of the members of this first group of settlers, Ellis Browne, received a grant for "Three Hundred Acres of Land ... for transportation of himself[,] Edward Stone[,] and John Macoben ... here to inhabitt in Anno 1649," proving that John Maccubbin, as his name was commonly spelled in Maryland, arrived as an indentured servant for Ellis Browne.[77] Browne's land was surveyed for him in October,1652, and was later sold to John Larkin, a prominent Quaker landowner, who called the property Larkinton.[78] This plantation evidently was in the South River area of Anne Arundel County and, later, may have become part of the 650-acres patented in 1663 and called Larkin's Hills.[79]

John Maccubbin must have worked as a servant on Browne's land grant, and he may have continued working there when it was sold by Browne to John Larkin. John may have been an indentured servant as late as 1656, depending on when he first signed his indenture contract.

He then would have been entitled by law to his freedom dues, "which in Maryland consisted of clothing, an axe and a hoe, and three barrels of corn, all due from the former master—and until 1681 a 50-acre land warrant obtainable on demand from the proprietor."[80] If John received land as part of his freedom dues, there is no surviving record that he had it surveyed and recorded in his name.

In the early years, until about 1690, the expanding tobacco economy of Maryland provided opportunities for enterprising young men, but tobacco culture was very labor intensive. "Seedlings, sprouted in a shady forest loam, had to be transplanted in early summer to the open field and cultivated frequently with a hoe. Harvesting was a matter of plucking and carefully drying each tobacco leaf" in a tobacco barn.[81] A man working in the tobacco fields tended about 10,000 plants covering 2-3 acres and produced about 1800 to 1900 pounds of tobacco per year.[82] After about three years, the soil was exhausted, and a new plot had to be cleared and planted.[83]

John Maccubbin must have been a strong man, because he survived the hard work and the disease-ridden environment of the tobacco plantations. Malaria, scurvy, and typhoid were endemic, and there were very few trained physicians.[84] "Over a third of servants arriving during the middle decades of the 17th century died before they completed their contract."[85] John not only survived the years as an indentured servant and independent planter but he lived to an age of about fifty-four years, "an age that only about one-quarter of immigrants attained."[86]

We do not know when John McCubbin first became an independent planter, but it was sometime before 1662, when he was living at "Maccubbins Cove," on the north side of the South River. Evidence for this is the 1662 patent for the tract Hamilton, which mentions "John Maccubins land" and "Mecubbins Cove" as bounding land.[87] John must have been producing tobacco there because, in October 1662, he was fined 500 pounds of cask tobacco for refusing to train with the local militia.[88] The land where John was living, at "Mecubbins Cove," was then part of the Brampton land grant, which John did not own until 1666 when he acquired it from Richard Beard.

The location of John Maccubbin's original plantation house is not known, but it probably was on Maccubbin's Cove, where he was living in

October 1662. The cove would have been a natural anchoring site for the boats that served his plantation. We don't know when he moved onto the higher ground, but his next house may have been near the much more recent Brampton manor house, built in about 1740 by John's son John, Jr. Because of the lack of roads, planters required access to water transport, and the early plantations were dotted along the shores of the coves and bays of the Severn and South Rivers. They rolled their casks of tobacco to the nearest dock where it could be taken onboard by a boat or ship.

A replica of a plantation owner's house at St. Mary's City, Maryland, now a state historic area, may be similar to the house occupied by John Maccubbin when he lived near Maccubbin's Cove on South River in 1662. (Photo by the author, June 2001.)

The dwellings and other buildings built by the early settlers were not meant to be long-lasting and have since melted into the ground. Houses at this time were small frame buildings, built on vertical wood posts buried in the ground without any other foundation, and covered with wooden siding. "Even as late as 1798, the mean size of a plantation house in Anne Arundel County consisted of one or two rooms measuring 24 by 30 feet." In some cases, there would be a separate kitchen (sometimes connected to the dwelling by a covered space called a "hyphen"), and perhaps a hen house, milk shed, and spring house.[89] There also would be a tobacco barn. Archeological studies in St. Mary's, the first settlement in Maryland, have uncovered the holes made by the vertical support posts, marking the size and shape of the buildings there. St. Mary's is now a state historic site.

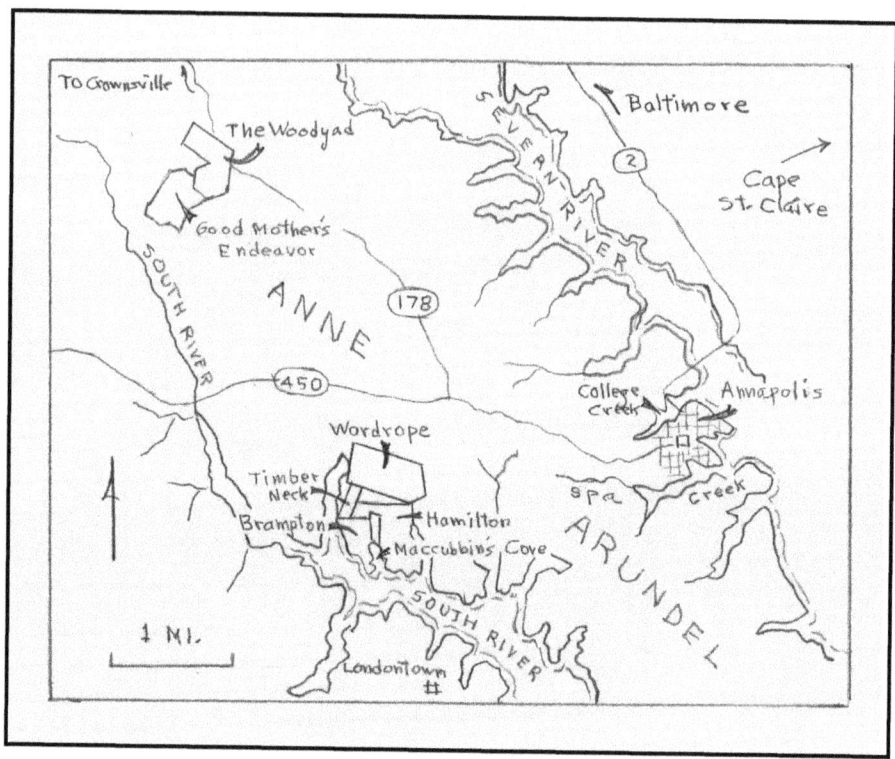

The patents Brampton, Timber Neck, and Wardrope, which John Maccubbin acquired between 1665 and 1675, were his original plantation lands, near his first home on Maccubbin's Cove. Hamilton and Young's Chance (between Brampton and Hamilton and not labeled here) were acquired later by other members of John's family. Woodyard and Good Mother's Endeavor were part of the original lands of the Howard family and were later owned by John Maccubbin's widow, Eleanor. (From Dorsey, 1958, map.)

Brampton, the Home Plantation

Between 1665 and 1675, John Maccubbin acquired the patents for the land that would become his home estate. His first patent, dated 1665, was for Timber Neck (40 acres), and the patent refers to boundaries with an adjacent "parcel of Land formerly laid out for the said Maccubbin," the land where he must have been living at the time.[90] On November 13, 1666, John Maccubbin purchased the patent Brampton (100 acres), which had been surveyed and patented for Richard Beard in 1659.[91] John presumably was living on Brampton with the consent of the Beard family, perhaps as a tenant farmer.

John acquired the bordering tract of Wardrope, 200 acres, on March 14, 1675. Wardrope was originally patented in 1663 by James Wardner, who sold it in 1671 to the widow Mary Gibbs, who married Alexander Gardner, who soon died. Mary Gibbs then, in 1675, sold the patent to John Maccubbin for a very small amount of money (2 shillings and 6 pence).[92] When he acquired Wardrope, John had consolidated the plantation lands of Brampton, Timber Neck, and Wardrope that would be owned by the Maccubbin family until 1791. John's grandson Richard Maccubbin would later add to the original plantation by acquiring the adjacent patent Hamilton in 1763.

The Beard, Wardner, and Gardner families, who owned the land later acquired by John Maccubbin, were among the early settlers who came to Annapolis from Virginia in 1649 with the group that included Ellis Browne and John Maccubbin.[93] Richard Beard, was a planter and a boatwright, and his son Richard, Jr. became a Justice and a Deputy Surveyor for Anne Arundel County.[94] The Beard and Gardner families, like John Maccubbin, are known to have become Quakers.

Another of the founding families that was that of Cornelius Howard and his sons, who patented their land in Anne Arundel County in the 1660s and 70s.[95] One of those sons, John Howard, Sr., was, like John Maccubbin, fined in 1662 for refusing to train with the militia and, therefore, probably was a Quaker.[96] Another son, Samuel Howard, married Catherine, the daughter of James Warner, whose second wife was Elizabeth Harris, the well-known Quaker missionary who converted many of the early immigrants to Quakerism.[97] John Maccubbin probably had an early and a close connection to the Howard family.

The Quaker Community of South River

The early settlers, probably including John Maccubbin, came to Maryland with strong religious underpinnings but, lacking ministers and churches, remained "unchurched". Maryland, unlike Virginia and other Royal colonies, was originally organized to welcome Catholics and other non-Anglicans and had no state-sponsored church. The Church of England did not become the "established" church of Maryland until 1692, when parish churches were built in Annapolis and South River.

When Elizabeth Harris and other Quaker missionaries starting visiting the Ann Arundel area in 1655/56, many of the local residents "willingly listened to preaching of the Gospel by the new sect."[98] It is estimated that seventy-eight of the founding families of Anne Arundel County, many of whom came the area as English Puritans, became Quakers.[99]

The Quakers traditionally practiced their religion without a minister or other "intermediary" between themselves and God and held their meetings in their houses or other informal meeting places.[100] Richard Beard and others were "convinced into Quakerism" at a meeting at Beard's house on South River in 1657.[101] "Beard's house" may have been at Brampton, which John Maccubbin did not formally own until 1666. It seems likely that John Maccubbin participated in these meetings with the Beards, Warners, Gardners, and other neighbors, perhaps including the Howards. Today, a street in the South River area near the historic Brampton plantation house is named "Friends Road", undoubtedly commemorating this early community of Quakers, the Society of Friends.

In 1658, the Council of the Province of Maryland ordered that the Quakers, if they would not take an oath of allegiance, should be expelled from the province.[102] A year later, the Council complained that Quakers were dissuading the people from complying with the militia acts and ordered that they be punished.[103] In 1662, a penalty for "obstinate refusal" was imposed by the Anne Arundel County Court, and it was at this time that John Maccubbin, John Howard, Alexander Gardiner (Gardner?), and other Quakers were fined 500 pounds of cask tobacco or two months imprisonment.[104] "At first their refusal to abide by the orders to which they were opposed, created much discontent, but their gentle manners soon brought friends."[105]

A description of these early settlers in Maryland is provided by George Alsop, a young man who wrote in the mid-1660s, as follows:

> "These Christian Natives of the Land, especially the [Men], are generally conveniently confident, reservedly subtle, quick in apprehending, but slow in resolving . . . The women differ something in this point, though not much. They [the women] are extremely bashful at the first view, but after a continuance of time hath brought them acquainted, there they become discreetly familiar, and are much more talkative than men. All Complemental Courtships . . . are meer strangers to them . . . so that he that intends to Court a Mary Land Girle, must have something more than . . . a long winded speech to carry on his design.
> "[And] the Son works as well as the Servant . . . so that before they [the sons] eat their bread, they are commonly taught how to earn it; which makes them . . . capable of receiving that which their Parents indulgence is ready to give them, and which partly is by their own laborious industry purchased."[106]

After 1696, when the Church of England (renamed the Episcopal Church after the American Revolution) became the state-sponsored church in Maryland, residents were required to pay a tax in support of the church. By this time, because of social and economic reasons, Quakerism was in decline.[107] Some of the former Quakers, including some of John Maccubbin's descendants, became supporters of St. Anne's Episcopal Church in Annapolis or All Hallow's Church in the South River area. Other Quakers became Presbyterians or joined the new faith of Methodism.[108]

John Maccubbin and his Wife or Wives

There are no official records of marriages or births in early colonial Maryland, but the date of John, Sr.'s marriage is believed to be about 1662 because the date of birth of his first child John, Jr. is calculated to be 1663.[109] In 1662, John would have been about 30 years old (assuming he was born in 1632). He was an independent tobacco planter living near Maccubbin's Cove on South River in a community of Quakers, on land that he did not yet officially own.

In 1662, the few women in the male-dominated society of Maryland would have come there as children with the early immigrant families. Because of the relative isolation of the community in which John lived, it is likely that his wife was a member of that community. Early historians who wrote about the founders of the Ann Arundel County area have suggested that John Maccubbin had two wives, the first of whom was a daughter of Samuel Howard and Catherine Warner, and that the second was the Eleanor named as his wife in his will, possibly a member of the Carroll family.[110]

The Howards and the Warners were among the families who came to Anne Arundel County in the 1650s from Lower Norfolk County, Virginia, where they were persecuted for their "nonconformist" (probably Puritan) beliefs. Matthew Howard and his sons acquired several large tracts south of the Severn River west of Annapolis, which they patented starting in 1664.[111] Samuel Howard, the eldest son, married Catherine Warner, the daughter of James Warner and Elizabeth Harris, the Quaker missionary, before 1673.[112] Samuel and Catherine Howard had several children, some of whom were born in Virginia and had traveled with their family to Maryland. One of Matthew Howard's other sons, John

Howard, Sr., married Susannah Stevens after arriving in Maryland and later married John Maccubbin's widow Eleanor after John died in 1686.

The main evidence that John McCubbin had a first wife, a daughter of Samuel Howard, is the will of Samuel Howard, whose son, John Howard, Sr. married Eleanor, John Maccubbin's widow. At the time of this marriage to Eleanor, John Howard, Sr. had one adult son, Phillip, who died in 1705. In his will, Samuel Howard named his grandchildren as Samuel, John, and Elizabeth Maccubbin. Another court document, evidently related to this will, affirmed cash benefits to John, Samuel, and Elizabeth, the "sons and daughter of John and Deborah Maccubbin."[113] Most early authors believe that Samuel's "grandchildren" were the children of John Maccubbin and that John's wife was Deborah Howard. A more recent author, Adolf Loeser, believes that these grandchildren were the children of John Maccubbin's eldest son John, Jr., but the timing of events make this seem very unlikely.[114]

Welsh, who wrote in 1928, believes that Samuel Howard had daughters Sarah and Susan, and that the daughter who married John Maccubbin was a third, older daughter whose name is unknown.[115] Newman believes that Samuel Howard had daughters Susan, Ruth, and Deborah.[116] If this Deborah Howard married John in about 1662, she would have been older than the daughters Susan and Ruth, and she would have been born in Lower Norfolk County before the Howards came to Maryland (born by 1645 if she was at least age 17 when she married John Maccubbin in 1662). Hugh Jenkins in his McCubbin genealogy, accepts that this Deborah Howard was the first wife of John Maccubbin and was the mother of some and perhaps all of the children.[117]

A recent writer, Adolf Loeser, believes that the Eleanor named in John Maccubbin's will was John's only wife and that her family origin is unknown.[118] Eleanor remarried after John died and lived until 1711, surviving him by twenty-five years, suggesting that she was much younger than John and was in fact his second wife. Welsh and others who believe that Eleanor was John's second wife also believe that she was a member of the illustrious Carroll family.[119] Again, the evidence is circumstantial, mainly the fact that Eleanor's will was witnessed in 1705 by Attorney General Charles Carroll, Sr., his wife Mary, and two nephews, and was proved in court by Charles Carroll, Sr., Charles Carroll, Jr., and

James Carroll in 1711.[120] This Charles Carroll, Sr. arrived in Maryland by 1688 to serve as Attorney General of Maryland and settled in Annapolis where he became one of the largest landowners in Annapolis.[121]

On the genealogical chart in Michael Trostel's book, "Mount Clare", Eleanor's last name is not shown, but a note there indicates that Eleanor Maccubbin was the "daughter of Anthony Carroll of Lissenboy County, Tipperary, and the first cousin of Charles Carroll of Annapolis, the Attorney General."[122] Trostel cites no evidence to support this relationship, but it is interesting to note that Charles Carroll of Annapolis was the eldest son of Charles Carroll the Settler, who witnessed Eleanor's will

Although the identity of John Maccubbin's wife or wives is uncertain, it seems likely that John had two wives and that the first probably was a daughter (Deborah?) of Samuel Howard and the sister of John Howard, Sr. It is less likely that John's wife, Eleanor, mentioned in his will, was a member of the Carroll family. This branch of the Carroll family was not in the Annapolis area before John died in 1686, and there is no evidence that any of the Carrolls were in the area in 1662 when John was married and started his family. Even so, it is clear that the McCubbins had close relationships with the Attorney General, Charles Carroll, at least as early as 1705, and with Dr. Charles Carroll and his son Charles Carroll the Barrister after 1747, when Nicholas, the grandson of John Maccubbin, Sr. married Mary Clare, the daughter of Dr. Carroll.

John Maccubbin and His Family

Although the identity of John Maccubbin's wife or wives is uncertain, this wife or wives provided him with seven children. The children and their approximate dates of birth are: John, Jr. (born 1663/1664); Sarah (born by say 1668); Samuel (born 1673); William (born say 1675); Eleanor (born 1677?); Zachariah (born about 1679); and Moses (born by say 1683/1684).[123] The sons are named in their father's will, and the daughters are named in the will of John, Sr.'s widow, Eleanor, or other documents. The dates of birth are calculated by Loeser from land records and wills and are generally consistent with those reported by other writers.[124]

The only official record of John Maccubbin, Sr.'s life, after the purchase of his land grants, is a court record showing that in April, 1679, he served on a jury of inquest called to determine what lands Thomas Hall owned.[125] The lack of other court records may suggest that John lived a quiet and private life on his plantation, raising his family in the local community of Quaker families, and avoiding any further conflict with the authorities. His plantation must have required all of the time and labor that he and his family could provide, but only John, Jr. and Samuel were old enough to have provided much help with the farm labor before John died. There is no evidence from property records or from John's will that he had any slaves.

When John Maccubbin died in 1686 at the age of about 54, his son John, Jr. was about 23 years old and his other children were all very young, between 13 and 2 years of age. John left a will that made his wife Eleanor the executer and immediate beneficiary of his estate. His son, John, Jr., the only son over 21 years of age, would receive "the plantation and Land whereon I now live [,] known by the name of Bramton being one hundred and forty ackers on the North Side of South River," but John, Jr. would not formally own this land until after Eleanor's death or remarriage. His other, much younger sons, Samuel, William, Zachariah, and Moses would receive "two hundred ackres of Land lyeing on the north side of South River known by the name of Wordrape [Wardrope]," to be divided equally among them when they are at age 21 or, if Eleanor remarries, at age 18. Daughters Sarah and Eleanor are not mentioned in the will, but John gave to Eleanor "my pesonall Estate and to be att her disposeing for the good of her children as she shall think fit."[126]

A Memorial Committee of the Colonial Dames of America reported in 1908 that "On the shore of South River, on his old plantation of Brampton, lie presumably the remains of John Macubin, or Mackubin, the original owner of the land in 1658, and the founder of the family in Maryland."[127] The old graveyard where John was believed to be buried was "intact and unmolested at the last visit of the chairman of the Memorial Committee but was overgrown with trees and brambles and bore no sign of having once served as a graveyard, save the oblong holes or indentations which mark the graves of those buried there."[128] A more recent owner of the property, James B. Lackey, who owned Brampton when the Maryland Trust nomination form was compiled, noted that "there is a small graveyard in the woods near the house."[129] When Brampton was eventually lost to the Maccubbin family in 1791, the land was transferred to the new owner except for "the family cemetery."[130]

Eleanor and Her Second Husband

After John Maccubbin, Sr.'s death in 1686, his widow Eleanor married John Howard, Sr. The date of her marriage to Howard is unknown, but it probably was soon after John Maccubbin's death because of the youth of some of her children and the difficulty of maintaining the plantation. In 1686, John, Jr. was about twenty-three years, but the other children were only about thirteen years old or younger. John, Jr. may have managed the plantation with his mother's help until she remarried and moved to the plantation of John Howard, Sr., at which time John, Jr. would have been legally entitled to inherit Brampton. Some or all of the other children may have lived with Eleanor at the Howard plantation.

John Howard, Sr. was, like John Maccubbin, a Quaker, and his family was close to the Maccubbin family. As discussed earlier, John Howard's older sister may have been John, Sr.'s first wife. Howard had married, first, Susanna Stevens in 1664-66 and was a widower with one son, also named John, when he married Eleanor. He and Eleanor had no children together. Like other members of the Howard family, John Howard, Sr. evidently valued the heraldry of his English forebearers, because his coat of arms is shown on the wax seal of his will.[131]

Eleanor and John Howard, Sr. probably lived on Howard's home plantation, consisting of the Woodyard, 160 acres, and Howard's Thicket, 50 acres, in Anne Arundel County a few miles north of Brampton. John Maccubbin, Jr. inherited Brampton when Eleanor remarried and he continued living there, but the other children may have lived with Eleanor at the Howard plantation. By the time John Howard died in 1695, Samuel and William may have moved away from home, but Zachariah, who was about 16 years old, and Moses, who was 11, must have continued living with Eleanor at the Howard plantation, which Eleanor inherited.[132] The will of John Howard, Sr. was witnessed by six persons, including Cornelius Howard and both Zachariah and William Maccubbin.[133]

In 1698, Eleanor Maccubbin Howard ordered a new survey of the Howard plantation, which showed that there were 185 aces of "surplus land." She then obtained a new patent which combined the Woodyard, Howard's Thicket, and the surplus land into one new plantation called Good Mother's Endeavor, 285 acres. In 1700, Eleanor, on her own, obtained a warrant for 400 acres of land on the Patuxent River in Prince George's County, Maryland.[134] She then evidently gifted this land, called Mother's Gift, to her oldest son John McCubbin, Jr., who also owned Brampton. Eleanor was remembered in the 1703 will of her stepson, another John Howard, who asked her to be the guardian for his daughter until her sixteenth birthday or the day of her marriage.[135]

Eleanor (Maccubbin) Howard, who had survived two husbands and her stepson, was still a relatively young and capable woman when, in 1705, she met with the attorney Charles Carroll to consider the best allocation of family resources and to write a will.[136] By this time, her son John Maccubbin, Jr. had become the owner of Brampton and Timber Neck, and her sons Samuel and Zachariah were married and lived on properties that had been inherited by their wives. The four younger sons each owned a share in Wardrope, as provided by their father's will and which they legally inherited when Eleanor remarried. It must have been decided by Eleanor and her family that the youngest son, Moses, should own all of Wardrope. To help accomplish this, the attorney Charles Carroll granted Moses a mortgage loan on his share of Wardrope, probably to provide the cash to pay his brothers Samuel, William, and Zachariah for their interest in the property.[137]

In her will, dated November 10, 1705, Eleanor made her daughter Sarah (Maccubbin) Reynolds the executor of her estate and provided for Sarah's four children by Sarah's first marriage to William Griffith. Eleanor bequeathed the land Howard's Thicket (by then renamed Good Mother's Endeavor) to her son William Maccubbin, who was then living there, probably with his younger brothers. She also reaffirmed in her will that the rights to Wardrope be released by Samuel, William, and

Zachariah to their brother Moses, by a deed which was recorded days after probate of her will.[138] Eleanor died in the summer of 1711, probably at her plantation Good Mother's Endeavor, and was buried on July 11, 1711, according to the records of St. Anne's Parish.[139]

By the time Eleanor died in 1711, the plantations were not as productive or as valuable as they had been before about 1690, when the market price of tobacco had declined substantially and the economy depended more on the growth of government and businesses in Annapolis after it became the provincial capital of Maryland. Some of the plantation owners sought other sources of income or took mortgages to maintain their properties. Also, there was no land available for the families of the early plantation owners to start new plantations. In some cases, these children and grandchildren moved to Baltimore or Prince George's Counties where there may have been better opportunities to acquire land and support their families.

Four of John Maccubbin, Sr.'s sons, John, Jr., Samuel, Zachariah, and Moses continued to be plantation owners for the rest of their lives, but some of their children and grandchildren moved into Annapolis where they and their children became successful businessmen and members of the establishment there. Another of John, Sr.'s sons, William, sold his share of McCubbin property and moved to Baltimore. It probably was this William or his son William, Jr., who then moved to new settlements in the Piedmont of Virginia and established the family line that continued to move west as new land became available.

John Maccubbin, Jr. the Eldest Son

John Maccubbin, Jr., the first-born son, was about 22-23 years old in 1686 when his father died at Brampton. Rudolf Loeser believes that John, Jr. married, first, a daughter of Samuel and Catherine Howard, and, second, Ann, whose last name is unknown.[140] Other authors believe, as discussed earlier, that it was John, Sr. and not John, Jr. who married a daughter of Samuel Howard and that the "grandchildren" named in Samuel Howard's will were the children of John Maccubbin, Sr. These authors believe, and I agree, that Ann was probably John, Jr.'s only wife.

The historic brick Brampton house, built in about 1740 by John Maccubbin's son John, Jr. near the site of John Maccubbin's original house on Maccubbin's Cove, has been partially modernized and is occupied as a private residence on Cape St. John Road. A sign in front of the house reads "Brampton." (Photo by the author, June 2001.)

John, Jr. and Ann had at least ten children, born between 1698 and about 1714. The names and birthdates of eight of them, Samuel, Deborah, Ann, William, Rachel, John III, Zachariah, and Moses, are recorded in the records of St. Anne's Episcopal Church in Annapolis. The two youngest children, Ruth and Richard, are named in their father's will.[141] Not much is known about many of the children, perhaps because they moved away from Anne Arundel County to start their own families. William moved to Baltimore County and married, first, Nellie Griffith, and second, Clara Whips, former wife of John Whips, on August 11, 1735.[142] Some McCubbin family historians have suggested that this William was the father of the William who married Eleanor Conley and moved to Virginia but have not been able to confirm this.[143]

John Maccubbin, Jr., like his father, was a planter, living on the plantation of Brampton (100 acres) and Timber Neck (40 acres), which he had inherited from his father after his father's wife, Eleanor, remarried. In 1700, John, Jr also acquired the plantation Mother's Gift (400 acres) from Eleanor, who had inherited it from her second husband John Howard, Sr.[144] In 1717, John, Jr. had Brampton resurveyed, and, in 1740, he obtained a new patent for Brampton.[145] It probably was at about this time, in 1740, that John, Jr. built the brick manor house that still stands near Maccubbin's Cove on modern maps. In 1740, some of his children were still quite young and would have been living with their parents at Brampton.

This house, called "The Old McCubbin House at Brampton" on the nomination form for the National Register of Historic Places, is still occupied as a residential property, set back from the street on a large wooded site at 320 Cape St. John Road, Annapolis.

According to the nomination form, the original part of the house is brick, with solid, 16" thick walls, and a brick chimney at each end. "It has two stories, one room deep and two rooms long with a center entrance and hall." Frame additions, including the kitchen, added in the late 19th and early 20th centuries, have more than doubled the size of the original house. "The stair, door moldings, plaster work, and mantels all appear to be 19th century work."[146] When Donald and Mary Anne McCubbin visited there in June 2001, new owners had just moved in and were doing some modernization, including adding a breezeway connecting the main house to the former carriage house. They were very interested in the history of the property and gave us a tour of the house, including the kitchen area. A sign on the street in front of the house proudly identified the property as "Brampton."

The South River Club, modeled after the rural English clubs of the 18th century, limits its membership to lineal descendants of the colonial founders of Anne Arundel County. John Maccubbin's son John, Jr. and his grandson Samuel probably were members. Club members still meet in the historic club house, built in 1742, shown here. From Ware, 1990. (Photo by the author, June 2001.)

There are surprisingly few records of John Maccubbin, Jr. and his wife Ann except for those concerning a boundary dispute in 1720 with his neighbor (who owned Hamilton), the new patent for Brampton in 1740, and the birth records of their children at St. Anne's Church. John, Jr. probably was a member of the South River Club. This club, which dates from about 1700, was modeled after the rural English gentlemen's clubs of the eighteenth century. Membership in the club is traditionally limited to twenty-five men, all lineal descendants of the colonial founders of the Annapolis and South River areas. A fire in 1740 destroyed the original clubhouse and the records of its members before that time, but the clubhouse was rebuilt in about 1742. It was listed in the National Register in 1972.[147] Today the South River Club claims to be the oldest continuously operating social club in America.

A notice in the *Maryland Gazette* records that John Maccubbin, Jr. died in May 1752 at the age of 88 years.[148] In his will, made almost seven years before his death, John, Jr. left to his wife Ann "the Plantation I Now Live on and all of the Lands and appurtances thereto Belonging [,] Being Brampton, Timber Neck, and Thirty Acres Thereto Adjoyning[,] for and Dureing her Natureal Life (in case She doth not Marry)[,] and after her Decease To my Son Richard Mackubin and to his heirs forever." John, Jr. also specified that "my Daughters Rachel and Ruth Mackubin Shall Live on the Plantation aforesaid With my said Son Richard Till they are Marryed."[149] By the time of John, Jr.'s death in 1752, most of his children had married and perhaps had secured their own properties and livelihoods.

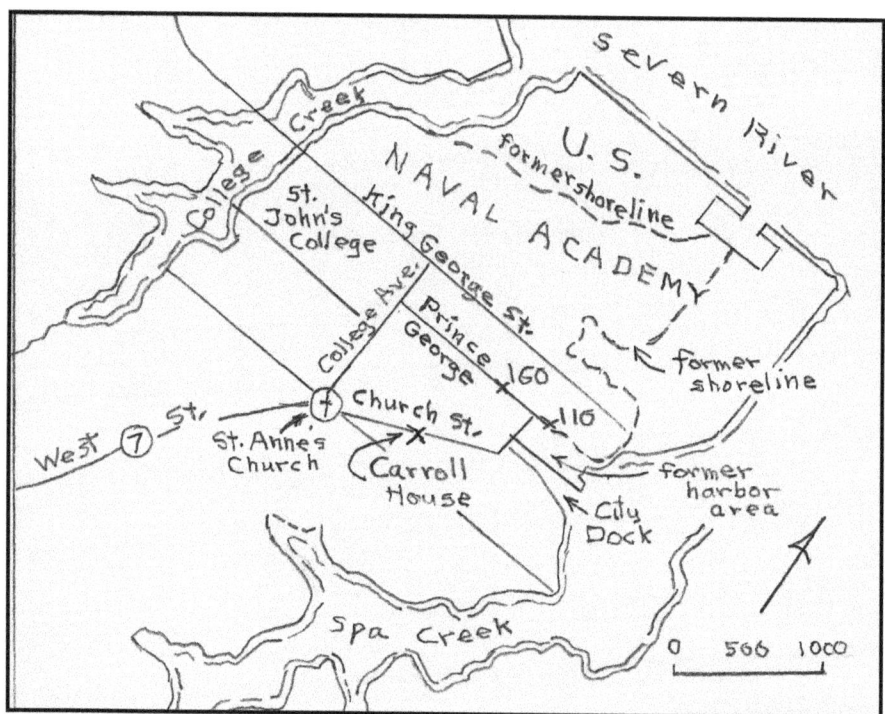

This map of downtown Annapolis, now a National Historic District, shows the location of the Carroll House, the Patrick Creagh house at 160 Prince George St., and the McCubbin-Patterson house at 110 Prince George St., all of which were occupied by members of the Maccubbin family between 1756 and 1786. Patrick Creagh's shipbuilding yard was located at the foot of Prince George St. on the original harbor (since partly filled in to provide a parking lot). (From Lindauer, 1997, Anderson, 1984, and Gary, 1953.)

Richard Maccubbin and the Merchant/Shipowner Patrick Creagh

John Maccubbin, Jr.'s youngest son, Richard, would eventually inherit Brampton, but only after his mother's death or remarriage. By 1747, Richard had become involved in shipping and trading ventures in Annapolis, and in about 1750 he married Elizabeth Creagh, daughter of Patrick and Alice Creagh, in Annapolis.[150] Patrick Creagh was a prominent merchant, builder, and shipowner in Annapolis.[151]

In 1730, Patrick Creagh purchased Annapolis town city lots 95, 98, and 99 on Prince George Street, and, by about 1735, he had built his dwelling house on lot 95.[152] In 1742 he contracted to build a new Governor's House but was unable to finish the project because of disputes over payment by the Maryland provincial government.[153] He did succeed in building the Old Treasury, which still stands, and other buildings in Annapolis. It is believed that Patrick built the mansion house Mount Clare near Baltimore for Dr. Charles Carroll, and that he also may have built the plantation house at Squirrel Neck on the Rhode River for Nicholas Maccubbin and Mary Clare Carroll.[154]

Patrick Creagh established his boat works at the foot of Prince George Street on the harbor, which was then larger than the present City Dock area, and he must have been building ships there by 1748 when the site was patented as Creagh's Discovery.[155] Patrick operated his ships in the tobacco trade with England as late as 1754, when his son James, who lived in London, was the commander of those shipping voyages.[156] Some of Patrick's ventures must have been very unprofitable, because he somehow became deeply indebted to merchants in London. In 1754 he mortgaged almost everything he owned, including his dwelling house in Annapolis, but no payments were ever made on those mortgages until after his death.[157]

It is not clear when Richard Maccubbin first became involved in trading and shipping in Annapolis. Records show that, from 1747 to 1758, he was Inspector of Customs for the Port of Annapolis, and that in 1769 he was one of five merchants who helped establish a "non-importation" association for the province of Maryland.[158] Like many of the other prominent businessmen in Annapolis, he was a supporter of St. Anne's Church, serving as a member of the church vestry and as a major subscriber to the rebuilding of the church after the earlier building was destroyed by fire in 1774.[159]

Richard Maccubbin inherited the family plantation on South River, which included the patents Brampton and Timber Neck, when his father died in 1752, but he did not acquire formal ownership until after his mother died. After Richard and Elizabeth were married in about 1750, they probably lived in Annapolis. In April, 1756, Richard purchased lot 24 and the house on it from Patrick Creagh, and Richard and Elizabeth Maccubbin may have lived there for a time.[160] This house on lot 24 was later razed to make way for the present Ridout house at 120 Duke of Gloucester Street, built in 1765.[161]

Patrick Creagh retained physical possession of his properties until his death in 1760, and it was not until then that Richard Maccubbin discovered the full extent of his father-in-law's financially fatal debts. Richard was able to absolve the estate of its entire indebtedness, largely by selling some land to meet the payments and to pay off the mortgages.[162] He then became owner of Creagh's land in the waterfront area at the foot of Prince George Street including the boatyard area, where he built a new street which he called "Creagh's Street" (now Craig Street on modern maps).[163]

The Maccubbin-Paterson House, at 110 Prince George Street, was owned by Richard Maccubbin and his son John Creagh Maccubbin. An addition has been added in the back, but the front part is the original brick house. Gary (1953) and Anderson (1984). (Photo by the author, June 2001.)

Richard Maccubbin assumed the mortgage on lots 98 and 99, building his own house there.[164] As mentioned before, this house no longer exists. The land was acquired by the Naval Academy, and the site of the house is on the parking lot adjacent to the Naval Academy Visitors Center. Lot 97 and the house on it, which was probably built by Creagh, was also acquired by Richard.[165] This house, now 110 Prince George Street, is now called the Patterson-Maccubbin house.[166] The former Creagh dwelling house on lot 95, however, was lost to Thomas Rutland, who acquired it at auction for 350 pounds on September 28, 1762.[167]

Richard Maccubbin died in 1779 and, in his will, named his wife Elizabeth and his four children, John Creagh, James, Elizabeth, and Richard, as heirs.[168] John Creagh and Elizabeth were the co-executors of the will.[169] Elizabeth inherited lots 98 and 99 and the house on them, where the Richard and Elizabeth lived at the time.[170] John Creagh inherited the Maccubbin family property on South River, then consisting of Brampton, Hamilton, Timber Neck, Duncans Luck, Young's Chance, and Hills Good Will.[171] Richard's wife Elizabeth died in 1800.[172]

John Creagh Maccubbin

John Creagh Maccubbin, the eldest son of Richard Maccubbin and Elizabeth Creagh (and the great-grandson of John, Sr.), was, like his father, an Annapolis merchant. He and his wife probably lived in his father's house on lots 98 and 99. John Creagh inherited Brampton from his father in 1779, but (for reasons that are not entirely clear) he mortgaged the property to Thomas Rutland, an Annapolis builder. In 1786, John Creagh purchased the former Patrick Creagh dwelling house on lot 95 from Rutland, paying more than the property was worth, perhaps as a way of paying off the debt.[173] He may have mortgaged Brampton in order to restore family ownership of the Creagh house and perhaps other properties. The mortgage on Brampton was acquired by another party, and in 1791 the Anne Arundel County Court ordered John Creagh to convey the Brampton patent to Allen Quiyn, the mortgage holder.[174] At this point the Brampton patent passed out of the hands of the Maccubbin family, although other parts of the original plantation remained in Maccubbin ownership.

Properties owned by Richard Maccubbin and perhaps by John Creagh Maccubbin included the house on lot 97, 110 Prince George Street, now called the Maccubbin-Paterson house. It is not clear whether this house was built by Patrick Creagh or by Richard Maccubbin, but it was adjacent to the former Patrick Creagh dwelling house later acquired by John Creagh Maccubbin. The front part of this L-shaped house is the original brick house, and the back part, now the dining room and kitchen, was added later.[175] In June 2002, when Donald and Mary Anne McCubbin visited this house, the owners graciously gave us a tour of part of the house.

The former Patrick Creagh dwelling house, now 160 Prince George Street, which was recovered to Maccubbin ownership by John Creagh Maccubbin in 1786, is now sometimes called "Aunt Lucy's Bakeshop." It was owned sometime after 1812 by John and Lucy Smith, a free black couple. John Smith operated a carriage and carting business out of the house, while his wife, "Aunt Lucy", was famous as a cook and had a bakeshop in the house.[176] It may be that John and Lucy (or perhaps Lucy's mother) were originally part of the Maccubbin household nearby at 110 Prince George Street.

James Maccubbin

James Maccubbin (or Mackubin, as he and his descendants spelled their name) was another son of Richard and Elizabeth and a great-grandson of John Maccubbin, Sr. James was born in about 1755 and married Martha Rolle in about 1783.[177] James owned land in Annapolis, which he inherited from his father, and may have been a merchant there. He also was a judge of the Orphans Court.[178] James and Martha and their four children lived on their property Bellefield, north of the Severn River. The tombstones at the family graveyard there bear inscriptions for James Mackubin, who died in 1834, aged 74 years, and for Martha Mackubin, who died in 1823, aged 63 years. Smaller stones in this graveyard are dedicated to the memory of their sons, James, who served in the War of 1812 and died in 1816, age 30 years, and Frederick, who in 1816 at age 28 years "was killed by a fall from his horse."[179]

When George Washington tendered his resignation as Commander-in-Chief of the Army at a meeting of the Continental Congress in Annapolis, he was given a reception at the assembly hall near the State House on the night of December 23, 1783.[180] On that great occasion, Washington chose Martha Mackubin as his partner to lead the Grand March opening the ball, perhaps because she was reputed to be "one of the most beautiful women of her day," according to an article in the *New York Times*.[181] Martha, the former Martha Rolle, was then "the twenty-year-old bride of James Mackubin of Annapolis."[182] This event is commemorated in a painting of Martha Mackubin and George Washington at the ball (illustrated in Magruder, 1931, p. xviii). Portraits of Martha and of her husband James, painted much later by Charles Willson Peale, hang in the house of Dr. J. Roland Walton, whose family is directly descended from Martha Rolle Mackubin.[183]

Zachariah Maccubbin of Brampton

Zachariah Maccubbin, born in about 1679 at Brampton, was a minor when his father John, Sr. died and his brother John, Jr. inherited the family plantation, Brampton and Timber Neck. Zachariah and his three brothers, Samuel, William, and Moses, inherited equal shares of the patent Hamilton but could not receive their shares until they reached maturity or after their mother's death. In 1704, Zachariah married Susannah, daughter of Nicholas and Hester (Larkin) Nicholson, in All Hallows Parish Church in South River.[184] Later, after 1707, Zachariah acquired Wyngates Rest (40 acres), Millhaven (191 acres), and a part of Mary's Mount (200 acres) by right of his wife Susannah.[185] He also owned Wilson's Grove, 200 acres, which evidently is where the main plantation house was located. In 1711, as discussed earlier, Zachariah and his brothers William and Samuel gave up their shares of the property Wardrope to their brother Moses, who by that time was old enough to receive his share under the terms of their father's will.

Zachariah probably was living at his plantation when, in October, 1730, he shipped sixteen hogsheads of tobacco to London on the ship Coeur Fidel.[186] He was one of the Justices of the Anne Arundel County Court in 1725.[187] He also served as High Sheriff of Anne Arundel County in 1724 and again from 1729 to 1732.[188] Zachariah's children Zachariah, Jr., Elizabeth, and Nicholas, were baptized at St. Annes in Annapolis, and Susannah, John, Ann and James were baptized at All Hallows Church in South River. Susannah, John, and James were buried at All Hallows.[189] Zachariah, like his brother John, Jr., was a member of the old South River Club, an English-style gentleman's club consisting of twenty-five of the local landowners, merchants, doctors, and clergymen, all lineal descendants of the founders. The clubhouse where the members met after 1742 still stands near Londontown, formerly a small seaport established in 1683.[190]

Zachariah Maccubbin outlived his wife, and in his 1753 will he bequeathed to his daughter Elizabeth Hood the plantation "on which she now lives, Wilson's Grove, 200 acres." To his daughter Susannah, who apparently was unmarried, he gave his bed and furniture, cows/calves, breeding ewes, sows/pigs, and corn and wheat. To his son Zachariah, Jr., he gave his land called His Lordships Manor and (presumably after his daughters were married) Wilson's Grove. He made his son Nicholas (who by then had moved to Annapolis and had married Mary Clare Carroll), the executer of his estate, and he asked to be buried at Nicholas's plantation, possibly Squirrel Neck.[191]

Nicholas McCubbin, Sr. and Mary Clare Carroll

Nicholas Maccubbin, Sr., youngest son of Zachariah and Susannah (and the grandson of John Maccubbin, Sr.), married Mary Clare Carroll on July 21, 1747, at St. Anne's Episcopal Church, Annapolis.[192] Mary Clare was the only daughter of Dr. Charles Carroll and Dorothy Blake Carroll and was the sister of Charles Carroll the Barrister.[193] Dr. Carroll was a member of the aristocratic O'Carroll family, which lost its lands in Ireland in the 1650s when "Cromwell's army swept across Ireland, confiscating the estates of all who resisted."[194] The Carrolls were Catholic and may have come to Lord Baltimore's colony because of the colony's "tolerance" of Catholics and other non-Anglicans. The first of the Carrolls to arrive in Annapolis was Charles Carroll the Settler, who arrived in 1688 to assume the office of Attorney General of the province.[195] This Charles Carroll was a distant relative of Dr. Charles Carroll, who arrived in Annapolis in about 1715.[196]

Dr. Charles Carroll married Dorothy Blake, a member of a prominent Catholic family. In 1723, he bought the lot and built the house on Church (now Main) and Conduit Street, where his children, Charles, Mary Clare, and John Henry were born. Dr. Carroll and his family lived in this house until 1746 when his son Charles Carroll returned from his education in England and assumed the title, Barrister, to distinguish himself from others with the Charles Carroll name.[197] Charles Carroll the Barrister married Margaret Tilghman in 1763 and had two children (twins) who died in infancy; they left no children.[198] Charles Carroll the Barrister was a very able speaker and writer, helped form the government of the state of Maryland, and served in the Maryland state senate.

The historic Carroll House was built in 1723 by Dr. Charles Carroll for his family and was occupied by Nicholas and Mary Clare Maccubbin and their son Nicholas, Jr. from 1746 to 1779 or later. It was moved from the corner of Main and Conduit Streets to its present location on the St. John's College campus. (From Anderson, 1984; photo by the author, June 2001.)

In 1746, the Carroll house on Church and Conduit Streets was sold to Nicholas Maccubbin, Sr., "a young Annapolis merchant ... who came from a family which had been established in Ann Arundel County for several generations." When Nicholas, Sr. and Mary Clare Carroll were married in 1747, Mary Clare returned to the house where she had been raised.[199] Although they acquired other properties, this house was the principal dwelling place of Nicholas, Sr. and Mary Clare and their son Nicholas Maccubbin, Jr. until 1779 or later, a period of more than 33 years.[200]

A sketch shows the Carroll house as it was in 1874 at its original location on Church and Conduit Streets, with the mouth of the Severn River in the distance.[201] It was a two-and-a-half story clapboard house, T-shaped, with three chimneys rising above the brick end walls.[202] The house was moved from its original site to its present location on the campus of St. John's College, where it has been partially restored and is now used as the admissions office of St. John's College.[203] A portrait of Charles Carroll, painted by Florence Mackubin (Maccubbin), a great-

great-great-niece of Charles Carroll, now hangs in what was probably the parlor of the house.[204] Another painting by Florence Mackubin, a portrait of Queen Henrietta Maria, for whom Maryland is named, hangs in the entry hall of the Maryland governor's mansion in Annapolis.[205]

In 1747, the year of their marriage, Nicholas, Sr. and Mary Clare Maccubbin purchased a 740-acre plantation called Squirrel Neck on the Rhode River, about 7 miles south of Annapolis. In 1748, they built a Georgian-style, five-part, brick house on high ground overlooking the Rhode River and Chesapeake Bay. Architectural details suggest that this house was built by the same builder as Charles Carroll's house at Mount Clare, in present-day Baltimore. The builder may have been Patrick Creagh of Annapolis.[206] The Squirrel Neck property was sold by Nicholas's son, James, to John Contee, and had several later owners. The house at Squirrel Neck was still standing in a 1971 photograph, but today all that remain are the brick chimneys.[207] The ruins of the house and the wharf on Chesapeake Bay that probably served the plantation are now on private property. Most of the rest of the former plantation property is part of an environmental research facility operated by the Smithsonian Institution.[208]

Nicholas, Sr. and Mary Clare probably lived at their house at Church and Conduit Streets for much of the time that he was a successful merchant in Annapolis. Records show that Nicholas succeeded his father Zachariah as High Sheriff of Ann Arundel County and served in 1733 and again in 1735.[209]. During the American Revolution, there were no battles in Annapolis, but troops of the Continental Army were stationed there.[210] Nicholas Maccubbin reportedly served in the Anne Arundel County militia and in the Maryland militia, but this may have been before the Revolution, when he was a young man.[211] Like other prominent citizens of Annapolis, he was a vestryman of St. Anne's Church and a large subscriber to its rebuilding in 1774.[212] He was a member of the lower house of the Maryland Assembly, and an Associate Justice for the district court.[213] Nicholas Maccubbin, Sr. died in 1787.

Nicholas, Sr. and Mary Clare had five sons (Nicholas, Jr., James, John Henry, Samuel, and Charles) and two daughters (Mary and Susannah). In his will, written in 1784, three years before his death in 1787, Nicholas, Sr. named his properties, including his plantations and mills and his lots and a brick warehouse in Annapolis. To Nicholas, Jr. he bequeathed his plantations Baldwin's Addition, Baldwin's Chance, and Brushey Neck. To James he gave the plantation Squirrel Neck, Annapolis city lot 47, and the house "where I lived" at Church and Conduit. To Samuel he gave extensive lands, mostly in the South River area.[214] The will was written shortly after Charles Carroll Barrister died and about the same time that Nicholas, Jr. and James changed their names to Carroll. Nicholas Maccubbin, Sr. must have planned that his assets be coordinated with those of Charles Carroll Barrister for the benefit of his family.

The house Mount Clare, in the city of Baltimore, was built in 1756 by Charles Carroll the Barrister, who later willed his estate to his nephews Nicholas, Jr. and James Maccubbin on the condition that they take the Carroll name. The manor house, furnished in period style, is now the Mount Clare Museum House. (From Trostel, 1981: photo by the author, June 2001.)

Brothers Who Changed Their Surname to Carroll

When Charles Carroll Barrister died in 1783, he left essentially all of his properties, including his home, Mount Clare, to his nephews Nicholas, Jr. and James Maccubbin (great-grandsons of John, Sr.) on the condition that they "take their mother's name of Carroll and that only, and use the Carroll coat of arms forever after."[215] The name change for the two Maccubbin brothers was made official by an act of the Maryland Assembly in 1783.[216] The very extensive Carroll estate included The Plains, west of Annapolis; several lots in the southeastern part of Annapolis; and Mount Clare and The Caves near Baltimore.[217]

In requiring the name change, Charles Carroll probably wanted to assure that his properties continue to be identified with the ancestral Carroll family and its heritage in Ireland. He probably also wanted to assure that those properties would be operated in an effective, business-like manner on behalf of his wife, who continued to live at Mount Clare until her death. He had transferred some of his properties to Mary Clare and Nicholas, Sr. earlier, after they were married in about 1747, and he must have been aware of the business experience of Nicholas, Sr. and his sons. Also, as mentioned before, it appears that when Nicholas, Sr. divided his assets among his sons in his will, he knew that Nicholas, Jr. and James would inherit other assets from Charles Carroll.

Nicholas (Jr.) Maccubbin Carroll married Anne Jennings, daughter of Thomas Jennings, the first Attorney General of the State of Maryland.[218] Nicholas, Jr. owned the 800 acres on South River that he inherited from his father and also 1000 acres in Kent County that he had been managing before his father's death.[219] Nicholas, Jr. and his wife made their home in Annapolis, on the site of the present public school, but he must have spent time at Mount Clare. A landscape painting of Mount Clare with the garden area in the foreground, by Charles Willson Peale, shows two horsemen thought to be Charles Carroll Barrister and his son-in-law Nicholas Maccubbin, Jr.[220]

Nicholas, Jr. was a member of the Lower House of the Maryland State Assembly from 1778 to 1785, representing Anne Arundel County. He also served as mayor of Annapolis in 1784-1785 and again in 1790-1791. He served on the Maryland convention that ratified the new federal constitution. He also was a Justice in Anne Arundel County, and an Associate Justice for the Third District Court.[221] A miniature portrait of Nicholas, Jr. on the Mount Clare website was reproduced there with the courtesy of the Hammond Harwood House Museum, Annapolis. Nicholas, Jr. died in 1812, before Margaret Carroll, Charles's widow, died at Mount Clare in 1817, so it was his brother James who moved to Mount Clare to assume management of the Carroll estate.

James Maccubbin Carroll and his wife, Sophia Gough, lived in the house at Church and Conduit Streets in Annapolis. James evidently was a merchant like his father and also invested in real estate, owning mortgages on many properties.[222] He served as a member of the Lower House and Senate of the Maryland state legislature between 1787 and 1799.[223] When James became the official owner of Mount Clare and moved there to assume onsite management in about 1817, he was 53 years old, and his wife Sophia had recently died.[224]. At about this time,

Portrait of James (Maccubbin) Carroll, who with his brother, Nicholas, Jr. inherited the Charles Carroll Barrister estate, moved into Mount Clare after the death of Charles Carroll's widow in 1817. (Photo by the author of the portrait on display in the Mount Clare Museum House in Baltimore.)

James sold the Annapolis house, and in 1825 he sold the plantation Squirrel Neck to John Contee. When James died in 1832, his son James, Jr. became owner of Mount Clare and other family properties. Portraits of James Maccubbin Carroll and his wife, Sophia, are reproduced in the book, *Mount Clare*, by Trostel.[225]

Samuel Maccubbin and Larkin's Hills on South River

Samuel Maccubbin, born in about 1763, did not change his name to Carroll as did his brothers Nicholas, Jr. and James (who, like him, were great-grandsons of John Maccubbin, Sr.). Samuel lived in the South River area on property that he evidently inherited from his father Nicholas, Sr. and in 1788 he married Mary Ann Rawlins, the daughter of Ann and Gassaway Rawlings. The Rawlings owned the estate of Larkin's Hills in the South River area, and the brick mansion house there is still preserved as one of the historic houses in Ann Arundel County. As mentioned earlier, Larkin's Hills, patented in 1663, may have included the land originally granted to John Browne for bringing John Maccubbin and another indentured servant to the area in 1649.

All Hallows Church on South River was built in about 1710, but an earlier church building on the site dates from about 1690 and is one the oldest churches in Anne Arundel County. Grave markers for Samuel, great grandson of John Maccubbin, and Samuel's wife Mary Ann are among those in the All Hallows churchyard. From Ware, 1990. (Photo by the author, June 2001.)

When Gassaway Rawlings died in 1812, Larkin's Hills was inherited by his daughter Mary Ann, who continued living there with her husband Samuel Maccubbin.[226] Samuel, like his grand-uncle, John, Jr. of Brampton, was a member of the South River Club, and both Samuel and Mary Ann were members of the All Hallows Episcopal Church, where Samuel was buried in 1838 and Mary Ann was buried in 1855.[227] All Hallows Parish records date back to 1688, and tradition has it that an earlier building stood at the site of the present church building as early as 1690.[228]

Moses Maccubbin, Youngest Son of John Maccubbin, Sr.

When John Maccubbin, Sr. died in 1686, his son Moses was a toddler. After his mother Eleanor married John Howard, Sr., Moses evidently grew up in the household of his stepfather at Good Mother's Endeavor and remained very close to the Howard family all of his life. John's will provided that Moses and his brothers should receive equal shares of Wardrope, but only when they reached the age of 21 (or 18 if their mother remarried). As discussed earlier, Moses received his share of Wardrope by 1711 and also, at that time, received his brothers' shares under the terms of Eleanor Howard's will.[229]

Moses was probably married by 1706, but the name of his wife is not known. He had three sons, Thomas, Moses, Jr., and Charles, named in his 1733 will, and three daughters, Elizabeth, Eleanor, and Mary.[230] The family undoubtedly lived at Wardrope, which apparently was a separate plantation, although originally a part of John Maccubbin, Sr.'s plantation on South River. A new survey, ordered by Moses, Sr., showed that the property had ninety-five acres more than previously known, and the new boundaries were confirmed in a new patent in March, 1725. This evidently triggered a boundary dispute with Samuel Young, owner of the adjoining property of Hamilton.[231] During the late 1720's, Moses, Sr., like his brother Zachariah, served as a Justice of Anne Arundel County Court.[232]

Moses Maccubbin, Sr. evidently transferred half of Wardrope to his son Charles, who in 1754 advertised: "To be sold: One Hundred and Fifty Acres of Land, called Wardrow, lying in Anne Arundel County, and within 4 miles of Annapolis, whereon is a Dwelling House, a Quarter, and a Tobacco House 40 Feet long, all new. The land is well wooded, and

Part of it will make good Meadow Ground. It lies upon navigable Water, and is chiefly under a good Fence of Chesnut Rails".[233] This part of the property, although advertised, was not sold and eventually became the property of Charles's son, another Moses, who owned a shop on Conduit Street, Annapolis, where he sold "cosmetics, soap, toothpaste, Powder Horns, combs, waters, pomades." [234]

In his 1784 will, Moses Maccubbin, Jr. bequeathed his part of Wardrope to his son William.[235] Thus Wardrope, part of the original plantation of John Maccubbin, Sr., the founder, stayed in the family for several generations.

William Maccubbin, Entrepreneur and Soldier.

William Maccubbin, son of John Maccubbin, Sr. and Eleanor, was born in about 1675, probably at Brampton, the family plantation on South River. He must have been an enterprising and independent-minded young man, perhaps much like his father John Maccubbin, the original immigrant. In 1694, William and three young partners were commissioned by the Maryland Assembly to build a fence to enclose the town pasture on the north side of Annapolis, where the townspeople could keep their horses. The work was completed by May 1695.[236] William evidently thought that the compensation he received was inadequate, so he petitioned the Maryland Assembly and was granted a larger amount.[237]

Records show that by August 1711 William Maccubbin was married to Jane, who signed a deed as his wife.[238] Some McCubbin genealogists (e.g. Hugh Jenkins) believe that this Jane was the daughter of William (or George) Westall and his wife Sarah Wade.[239] This Westall was presumably the son of George Westall, Sr., one of the original immigrants, who came to Maryland "before 1658" and secured a grant of 800 acres "for his own immigration and the transporting of his son George, and six other persons." He named his plantation "Scorton," and it was on this land that the port of Londontown was laid out.[240] William Maccubbin later owned a lot in Londontown which, in 1714, he transferred, with his wife Jane's consent, to his sister Eleanor Rumney, who was then a widow.[241] This may support the idea of a connection to the Westall family.

By 1707, Wiilliam Maccubbin probably lived at Good Mother's Endeavor, which he inherited in 1711 from his mother Eleanor, then the widow of her second husband John Howard, Sr.[242] Good Mother's

Endeavor consisted of the earlier patents of Howard's Thicket and The Woodyard, early plantation properties of the Howard family, northwest of Annapolis near the present town of Crownsville in Anne Arundel County. William Maccubbin was a witness to the will of John Howard, Sr., and he remained very close to the Howard family. Sometime between 1708 and 1714, he and his brother-in-law Edward Rumney were godfathers to the children of Cornelius Howard, one of the brothers of John Howard, Sr.[243]

Other records show that in 1709 William Maccubbin shipped tobacco to London. In 1714 he served on a jury, and in 1719 and 1721 he witnessed deeds in both Anne Arundel and Prince Georges Counties.[244] Then, in August 1724, William and Jane mortgaged Good Mother's Endeavour to secure a four-year loan that was recorded in Anne Arundel County.[245] After 1724, when William was 49 years old, nothing much is really known about him. He and Jane may have moved to Baltimore, but no records have been found to prove this .[246]

A "Capt. William McCubbin", who was reported in the letters to the editor of the *Baltimore Sun* to have been an "Indian fighter" and an officer of the militia, may have been this William Maccubbin, husband of Jane.[247] As noted by Adolf Loeser, this Capt. McCubbin could have been a colonial ranger, "guarding the frontiers against Indians in the mid-1690s" when he was a young man, presumably still living in Anne Arundel County.[248]

William and Jane evidently had at least two children: first, Eleanor, who is said to have been born in 1708 and married John Brewer IV by 1728, and, second, John, said to have been born in about 1709 and married Martha Ridgely, daughter of William and Jane Ridgely by 1732.[249] Anne Arundel County church records show that the son John who married Martha Ridgely had six children, including a William Maccubbin, born November 29, 1732.[250] Some family genealogists believe that this William (the son of John and the grandson of William and Jane) was the William who married Eleanor Conley in about 1747 and moved to Pittsylvania County, Virginia, in about 1755 when Eleanor is named as William's wife in a property transaction. This William would have been about 15 years of age if he married Eleanor in 1747, as some records seem to indicate, and 23 or younger if he married her by 1755, when she was listed as relinquishing her property rights as the wife of William.

Another McCubbin genealogist, Hugh Jenkins, suggests that William and Jane Maccubbin had a third child, also named William, and that this child was the William who married Eleanor Conley in Baltimore County in about 1747 and moved to Pittsylvania County, Virginia, in about 1755.[251] Assuming that this son William was at least 20–30 years old when he married Eleanor in 1747, he would have been born between 1717 and 1727 and his father William would have been between about 42 and 52 years of age at the time son William was born.

From this analysis, I conclude that the William who married Eleanor "Nellie" Conley in Baltimore County, Maryland, may have been either a son or a grandson of William and Jane Westall and the grandson or great-grandson of John Maccubbin, Sr., the founder, but we probably will never know his ancestral origins for certain because of the lack of records. Whatever his origins, records do show that this William acquired the land Strawberry Plains from Enoch Conley in 1747, and then sold this same land to Enoch Conley of Lancaster County, Pennsylvania, in 1748. These records identified William as Enoch Conley's son-in-law.[252] In November 1755, William sold Stansbury Plains (100 acres) near Little Pipe Creek—his wife Eleanor relinquishing her dower rights in this transaction.[253] It seems clear that, by this time, William and Eleanor were married and had children, but the births of these children are not well documented. It probably was shortly after this 1755 land transaction that the family moved to Pittsylvania County, Virginia.

Part III: American Homesteaders

Pittsylvania County, Virginia

Settlers began moving into the lush hills and valleys of the south-central Virginia Piedmont in 1738, when the British Crown and the Virginia Council began granting land there.[254] Early settlers included German, Quaker, and Scots-Irish immigrants who were then moving in great numbers from Pennsylvania down the Valley of Virginia and through the gaps in the Blue Ridge Mountains into the Piedmont region of Virginia and North Carolina.[255] The early settlers also included members of the established families of Tidewater Maryland and Virginia, probably because they were seeking cheaper land where they could establish new plantations.[256] Some of the earliest settlements were in Rockingham County, North Carolina, and just north across the border in Pittsylvania (formerly Halifax) County, Virginia near the future town of Danville. Plantation owners in Tidewater Virginia were content to allow the immigrants to settle in the area and provide a buffer against Indian raiders from the mountains to the west.

From 1757 until 1764, when the French and Indian War ended, the settlements of the Virginia Piedmont were under the threat of attack by Indians from the mountains to the west.[257] To defend against these attacks, a line of forts was built along the western margin of the settlements. Local militia forces manned these forts, and "colonial rangers" patrolled the area.[258] One of these forts was just west of the present town of Danville, Pittsylvania County, Virginia, where William and Eleanor McCubbin and their family settled and established a plantation in about 1755.[259]

Another early settler was John Fuller Lane, who moved with his family from Baltimore County and patented land in Pittsylvania County starting in 1746.[260] Dutton Lane, one of the younger sons of John

Fuller Lane, became an itinerant preacher and, in 1760, established the Separate Baptist Church, one of the first churches of any denomination in Pittsylvania County. In 1772, Dutton Lane's sister, Sarah, married Zachariah C. Maccubbin, son of William and Eleanor McCubbin, possibly in her brother's church.[261] The William McCubbin family had moved from the Baltimore area and arrived in the Danville area at about the same time as the Lane family, and it is possible that the McCubbins and the Lanes knew one another in the Baltimore area.

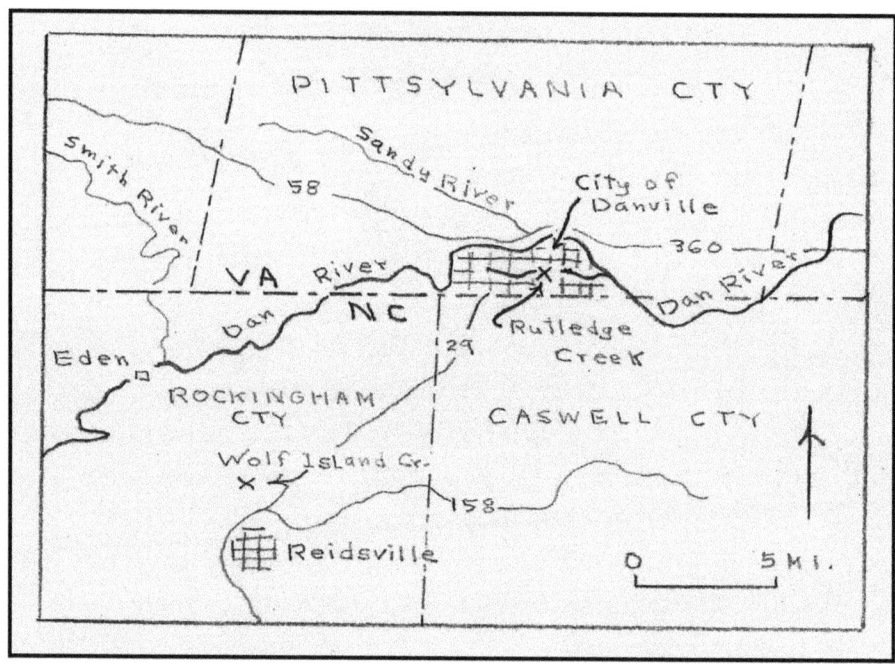

A plantation on Rutledge Creek (now within the city limits of Danville) in Pittsylvania County, Virginia, was the home of William and Eleanor McCubbin when their sons served in the American Revolution. Land which sons James P., Nicholas, and John McCubbin claimed on Wolf Island Creek north of the present city of Reidsville in Rockingham County, North Carolina, is now a golf course and housing development, but the Wolf Island Baptist Church and Cemetery survive nearby.

William and Eleanor Conley McCubbin in Pittsylvania County

When William and Eleanor McCubbin arrived in Pittsylvania County after about 1755, they were able to purchase land from other early settlers, as shown by county land records. William acquired 435 acres on the Rutledge Creek of the Dan River, now within the city borders of present-day Danville, Virginia, and near the border with North Carolina. There, he and his family established a farm or plantation where they probably grew tobacco. (The Danville area is still the center of the tobacco economy of the United States.) There are no records of their life on this farm except for county tax records, which show that, in 1787, William paid personal property taxes on "two horses and three cattle."[262] William and Eleanor evidently lived on this 435-acre property on Rutledge Creek until February, 1788, when it was sold.[263]

William and Eleanor McCubbin had five sons: John was born in about 1750, Zachariah C. (Conley?) on April 15, 1752, and James P., Sr. on April 4, 1755, all in Baltimore County, Maryland. Their son Nicholas was born January 8, 1760 and William P. was born in about 1762, after the family moved to Pittsylvania County.[264] The younger sons, Nicholas and William P. McCubbin, evidently lived with their parents at their home on Rutledge Creek during the early years of the American Revolution, when records show that they served their country as "commissaries" at a hospital there.

Later, Nicholas, James P. and John served in the North Carolina militia and, after the war, moved to Guilford (now Rockingham) County, just across the border in North Carolina. On February 16, 1788, William and Nellie sold their 435 acres on Rutledge Creek.[265] There is no evidence that they moved to Guilford County with their sons. It is not known where they died and were buried.

Sons of William and Eleanor McCubbin and the American Revolution

Zachariah C. McCubbin, son of William and Eleanor (Nellie) McCubbin, married Sarah Lane on December 6, 1772, in Pittsylvania County, Virginia.[266] Sarah, born in 1754 in Virginia, was the daughter of John Fuller Lane, who, with his brothers, had arrived in the area from Baltimore, Maryland, and patented land along Elkhorn Creek in 1746 and 1748, at about the same time that the McCubbins had arrived in Pittsylvania County.[267] Sarah Lane's brother, Dutton Lane, was the founder, in 1760, of the Dan River Baptist Church in what is now the town of Danville and was its pastor for many years.[268] Zachariah and

Sarah, and perhaps other members of the McCubbin family, must have been members of this church.

Although Zachariah C. McCubbin apparently was living in Pittsylvania County, Virginia at the time the Revolutionary War began, he evidently still had connections in the Baltimore area. He served as a captain in the militia of the Baltimore Town Battalion, and enlisted some 30 men to serve in his company.[269] Captain Zachariah's company, together with other companies from Baltimore, were formed into a battalion of the Continental Army in May, 1776.[270]

After the war, by October 11, 1783, Zachariah C. McCubbin was in Washington County, North Carolina (now in Tennessee), where he bought 200 acres from John Lane, possibly his brother-in-law.[271] Zachariah died in 1834, at age 82, and was buried in the Old Irish Cemetery in Tazewell, Claiborne County, Tennessee. His tombstone there reads: "Zachariah McCubbin, Maryland, Capt., Maryland Militia, Revolutionary War, April 15, 1752-Oct 24, 1834."[272] After Zachariah's death, his widow Sarah Lane claimed a letter of dismissal from the Big Spring Baptist Church in Tazewell and reportedly moved to Indiana. She was buried at the Old Irish Cemetery in Tazewell, Tennessee.[273]

Nicholas McCubbin probably was living with his father and mother, William and Nellie, in the early years of the Revolutionary War, when he served as "Assistant Commissary" to the Pittsylvania General Hospital.[274] A "commissary" was in charge of purchasing supplies, probably, in this case, for military use. In the spring of 1779, Nicholas volunteered to serve in the North Carolina militia for a term of nine months under Capt. John Davis and Lieut. George Pierce. On June 20th he fought in the battle of Stono Ferry in South Carolina. In the winter of 1780-1781, he volunteered for six months in Col. Culp's company and was stationed in South Carolina.

Nicholas testified to his military service in his pension application and stated that during the war he was living, presumably with his family, "about half a mile from Perkins Ferry on the south side of the Dan River."[275] He was married, first, in Pittsylvania County, in about 1785, to a person unknown, and, second, to Nancy Jones on December 22, 1798.[276] At the time of the 1790 census, Nicholas was living in his own household in Guilford (Rockingham) County, North Carolina.

James P. McCubbin, Sr., another son of William and Nellie, was living with his parents in Pittsylvania County, Virginia, when the Revolutionary War began. Court records show that, like his brother Nicholas, he served as Assistant Commissary at General Hospital in Pittsylvania County.[277] James P. volunteered with the North Carolina militia in the year 1776 or 1777 and served in a company under the command of Captain Pierce for a tour of six months. He took part in the Battle of Stono Ferry, south of Charleston, South Carolina, in June 1779, as the British were retreating to their base in Savannah after failing to capture Charleston. It appears that James and his brother, Nicholas, served together in the same unit during this battle. James's military service was documented in testimony at a court hearing in Green County, Kentucky, in March 1857 for Mary (McCubbin) Dicken, James's widow, to support her claim for pension benefits.[278]

John McCubbin, who married Sappho London, is not well documented.[279] He was born in Baltimore County, Maryland in about 1750, and probably was a son of William and Nellie McCubbin. A John McCubbin is listed in the 1740 U.S. Census in Baltimore County,[280] but there were other McCubbins in Baltimore County at the time.[281] Some family historians apparently believe that this John was the son of the William Maccubbin who married Clara Whips in 1735, and who, in turn, was a son of Samuel, the son of John Maccubbin, Jr.[282] It seems more likely that John was a son of William and Nellie McCubbin and that he and Sappho moved directly from Maryland to North Carolina, where he acquired land in Rockingham County after the war.[283]

Rockingham (Guilford) County, North Carolina

After the British announced their "southern strategy" to win the Revolutionary War, the British commander General Cornwallis established his base in Savannah, Georgia. He attempted to capture Charleston but failed, and during his retreat he was attacked by American forces, including at Stono Ferry in South Carolina. North and South Carolina became a crossroads of action during the war, and several decisive battles were fought there, including the Battle of Guilford Courthouse. American General Nathaniel Greene stationed his army, which included Virginia and North Carolina militiamen, on the north side of the Dan River near present-day Danville, Virginia. In March 1781, Greene moved south and confronted Cornwallis near the Guilford Courthouse, in present-day Greensboro, North Carolina. In this battle, Greene lost the field in the battle, but Cornwallis suffered so many losses that he withdrew to the Carolina Coast.[284]

During the Revolution, citizen soldiers from southern Virginia, North Carolina, and Tennessee left their families and their homes to fight in a battle or a campaign and then returned home with their guns and horses to tend their farms when that battle was over. As discussed above, these soldiers included the sons of William and Nellie McCubbin and were among the war veterans who moved their families across the state border to Rockingham County, North Carolina, and acquired land on the Wolf Island Creek area, just north of the present-day town of Reidsville.

We don't know when James P. McCubbin, Sr. moved to Rockingham County, but he was there by December 29, 1784, when he married Mary "Polly" Cook, probably at the Wolf Island Baptist Church. This church, founded in 1777, was one of the first churches in the area, and Isaac Cantrell was its pastor for over 20 years. "According to tradition, the original church was a six-sided log structure without windows and with log benches which sat on an earthen floor."[285] The number of members of the Wolf Island Church was thirty in 1790 and had increased to thirty-nine in 1793.[286] "For many years after settlement, wolves remained in isolated sections along the creek and occasionally their howls could be heard during the church services."[287] James P. McCubbin, Sr. and "Polly" and other members of the McCubbin family who lived in the Wolf Island Creek area probably were members of this church.

Nicholas McCubbin may have been the first of the brothers to acquire land in the Wolf Island Creek area. Deed abstracts show that Nicholas acquired 238 acres on Wolf Island Creek from William Patterson in 1787,[288] but he evidently sold this land in 1792.[289] He then purchased 300 acres on Wolf Island Creek in 1793.[290] Nicholas's brother, James P. McCubbin, Sr., acquired 200 acres on Horsepen Creek in September,1797.[291] The land on the north side of Wolf Island Creek is now occupied by the Wolf Creek Golf Club and a housing development. The Wolf Creek Primitive Baptist Church and Cemetery are located less than a mile south of Wolf Island Creek at the intersection of Wilson Road and Wolf Island Road. A sign in front of the church states that the church was established in 1777 and that the present church building was built in 1946. Death dates on the gravestones in the churchyard cemetery are as old as 1768.

James P. McCubbin, Sr. and Mary Polly Cook had thirteen children: John, born May 15, 1785; James P., Jr., born July 10, 1789; Sally, born September 19, 1791; Zachariah, born June 2, 1794; Joseph, born February 27, 1796; Mary, born August 24, 1798; William R., born July 16, 1800; Eleanor, born October 26, 1802; Pleasant, born September 19, 1804; Nicholas, born August 6, 1806; Thomas, born July 2, 1809; Martha Elizabeth, born September 8, 1811; and David, born September 22, 1813.[292] All were born in Rockingham County, North Carolina, except the four youngest, who were born after the family moved to Kentucky.

In the first U. S. census, in 1790, the households of the brothers James, Nicholas, and John are listed in the Salsbury District, Rockingham County. According to this census, James P. McCubbin, Sr. and wife had two sons under 16 years of age and no daughters. Nicholas and wife had six sons, all under 16 years of age, and two daughters, ages not given. John and wife Sappho had one son, under 16 years, and three daughters, ages not given.[293] The son would have been Nicholas ("Blind Nick") McCubbin, who later married Elizabeth "Betsy" Bloyd.[294]

John McCubbin and his wife Sappho London may have moved directly from Maryland to North Carolina, where John served in the militia and acquired land in the Wolf Island Creek area, Rockingham County, in 1783.[295] In his will, which was recorded in Rockingham County in 1809, John left "to my loving wife [Sappho] all of my whole estate during her natural life or widoehood. If she should marry, then she is to have the use of the plantation during her life and at her death, my will is that all my whole estate to be equally divided amongst all my children that is now with me, except one cow and calf to my daughter [in-law], Elizabeth [Betsy] Bloyd."[296] The Bloyds, who were neighbors at the time of the 1790 census, later moved with the McCubbins to Kentucky, and continued to be associated with them in Illinois.

Except for John, the McCubbin brothers sold their land in Rockingham County, North Carolina, over a period of time, before they moved to Green County, Kentucky in about 1806. When they made the move, James P. McCubbin, Sr. was 51 years old, his wife Mary Polly was about 37, and their children ranged in age from 2 years to 21. John and James P., Jr., who were the oldest children, at 21 and 17, must have been very helpful in making the difficult move to Kentucky. The brother John McCubbin evidently came back later to settle his will and sell his land in Rockingham County.

Green County, Kentucky

James P. McCubbin, Sr. and Family

After the American Revolution ended and land became available for settlement in Kentucky, pioneers from southwest Virginia and North Carolina followed the route through the Cumberland Gap, the

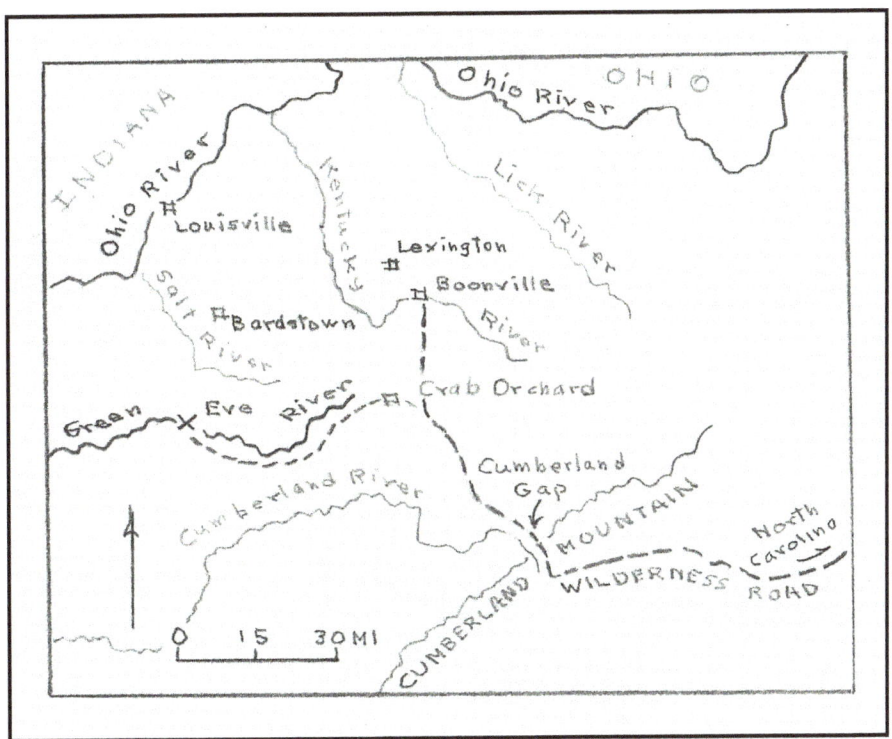

The Wilderness Road from southwest Virginia through Cumberland Gap into Kentucky, pioneered by Daniel Boone, was followed by the James P. McCubbin, Sr. party in 1806 as far as Crab Orchard where they turned west to follow the Green River to their new homes near Eve in Greensburg County. (Modified from Rouse, 2008, p. 134-135)

Wilderness Trail, established by Daniel Boone. By 1790, when the first United States Census was taken, nearly 70,000 people "had climbed on foot or on horseback that steep path."[297] After Kentucky became a state in 1792, the trail through the Cumberland Gap was widened, and the stream of immigrants increased. In 1806, according to family tradition, the family group led by James P. McCubbin, Sr. traveled this route from their homes in Rockingham County, North Carolina to Green County, Kentucky. They must have traveled the Wilderness Trail to the present town of Crab Orchard and then down the Green River to southcentral Kentucky, a distance of about 400 miles.

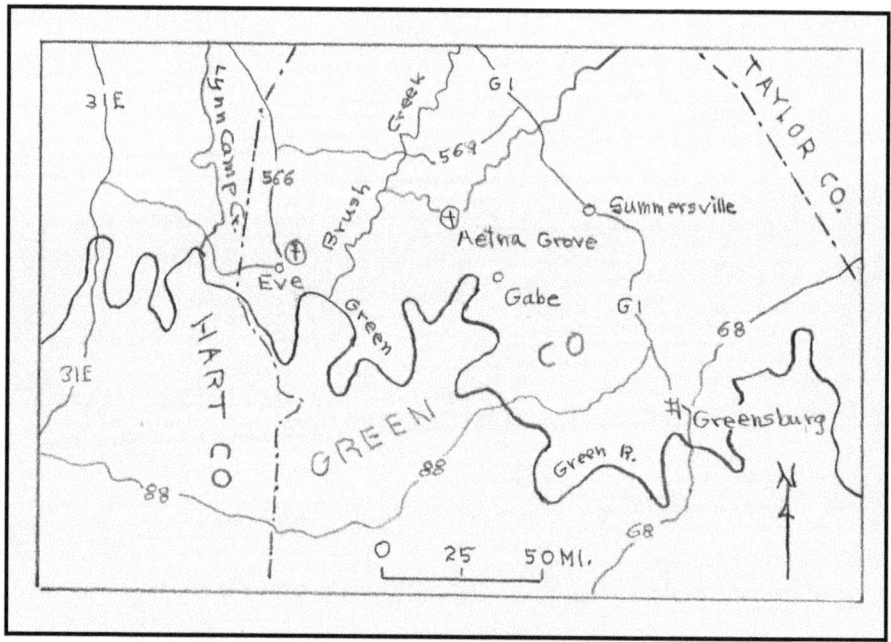

The townsite of Eve, on the north side of the Green River near Lynn Camp Creek and Brush Creek, was the location of the farms of the McCubbin families after they arrived in 1806. Greensburg, which became the county seat in 1793, was the nearest town and supply point.

Hunters and trappers from Virginia and North Carolina were in Kentucky long before Daniel Boone led the first group through the Cumberland Gap. They were called "long hunters" because they were away from home for months or even years.[298] According to one story, a party of long hunters had their camp in Green County plundered in their absence by "a half-breed Cherokee" in 1771.[299] Another story, reported by family historian Gleason McCubbin, is that a party of long hunters met their guide, Ben Lynn, where they camped at a creek on the Green River now known as Lynn Camp Creek.[300] The confluence of Lynn Camp Creek and the Green River is the location of a ford on the Green River and is near the settlement of Eve, where members of James P. McCubbin, Sr. party established their farms.

County government was first established by the Kentucky legislature in 1780-1784, and settlers, many of them Revolutionary War veterans, began arriving shortly afterward. Green County, named for the war hero General Nathaniel Greene, was formed from parts of Lincoln and Nelson Counties, and the town of Greensburg became the county seat in 1793. After arriving in the area in 1806, James P. McCubbin, Sr. and Mary Polly Cook McCubbin settled just north of the Green River between Brush Creek on the east and Lynn Creek on the west, near the present Vance-McCubbin cemetery. Their oldest sons, John, then 21 years old, and James P., Jr., 17 years old, took up their own land nearby. The other children, all less than 15 years old, lived on the farm with their parents. Other members of the McCubbin family settled on their own land nearby. Nicholas "Blind Nick" McCubbin, son of John and Sappho McCubbin, and his wife Elizabeth Betsy Bloyd settled a few miles away near Brush Creek and Little Brush Creek. Their son, Jim "Timberhead" McCubbin, and his wife Elizabeth Edgar settled just south of Eve, near the Green River.

Veterans of the Revolutionary War were offered land grants by the state of Kentucky, and after 1795 any settler could claim between 100 and 200 acres after they had lived on the land at least a year.[301] James P. McCubbin, Sr., and his son, James P. McCubbin, Jr., had been living on their homesteads for several years before they received formal ownership. James P., Jr. received ownership of his 140 acres at Eve on May 11, 1811. James P. McCubbin, Sr.'s land grant of 150 acres was surveyed on November 24, 1815, and the grant was signed on April 23, 1817 by the Lieutenant Governor of Kentucky.[302] The homesteads at Eve are now eighteen miles from Greensburg by way of Eve Road, the Hudgins Highway, and Summersville. Greensburg would have been the nearest source of supplies for the settlers near Eve.

Children of James P. McCubbin, Sr. and Mary Polly Cook were married between 1811 and 1828 in Kentucky, except for the three youngest who were married after they moved to Hancock County, Illinois.[303] James P. McCubbin, Jr. married Mary Parthenia Cook, daughter of Wiliam Cook, on October 26, 1813, shortly after he had established his farm in Green County. Eleanor McCubbin married William H. Rupe in 1823.[304] William H. Rupe was a grandson of Bernard Rupe (Roop), a German of Swiss descent, and a son of Barnett Rupe and Sarah Craven of Rockbridge County, Virginia. William H. Rupe served in the Revolutionary War, and in 1836 received a state grant of 60 acres "in the County of Green in the waters of Lynn Camp Creek." [305] William H. Rupe and Eleanor later pioneered with the McCubbin-Rupe party in Illinois.

The citizens of the community near Eve, where several branches of the McCubbin and associated families lived, may have held church services in their homes or in some temporary shelter. James P. McCubbin, Sr. was evidently a lay preacher (probably Baptist), and some of the McCubbin family histories refer to him as "Reverend James McCubbin." [306] Some family members also described James as a "gentleman farmer, schoolmaster, and preacher."[307] Today, the nearest church, the Aetna Grove Church, is less than 2 miles north of Eve.

Like other farms in the area, the McCubbin farms probably grew tobacco and cotton, which were transported down the Green River by flatboat to the markets in New Orleans. Life on the farms was described by one of the sons, Joseph McCubbin, to his grandson, Thomas Cameron McCubbin, as follows: "The Hawkins and McCubbins in KY were gunpowder makers besides farmers. The old kettles and grinders were long in existence. There grew some kind of trees along Green River & Lyn Camp River that were excellent charcoal for gunpowder making that was then was done by hand and the finishing touch was in reducing it to granules by running it through a coffee mill." Later, one of these coffee mills was taken to new settlements in Hancock County, Illinois, by Joseph McCubbin and was still in use there as late as 1888.[308]

On February 12, 1823, probably in anticipation of his death, James P. McCubbin, Sr. sold his 150 acres of land and its improvements to his son, Zachariah, for four hundred and fifty dollars.[309] Joseph, who moved to Illinois in 1834, was "always proud of the fact that his father, James McCubbin, had served in the Continental Army during the

Revolutionary War and would often relate stories which his father would tell concerning his army life. I asked him how long his father was in the service and he replied that he did not know, but he knew that he was still in the army when Lord Cornwallis surrendered."[310]

James P. McCubbin, Sr. died on March 16, 1824. His will, written on July 3, 1823 and proved on April 19, 1824 in Green County, left "unto my beloved wife [Mary] Polly McCubbin all my estate consisting in horses, cattle, hogs and household furniture, together with the possession of my land and divided amongst mine and her children after her death to wit —John, James, Thomas, Patsy, and David, and I do hereby leave my wife, Polly, sole executrix to this my will without giving security unto you for the performance of her duty herein."[311] The will was witnessed by his sons Nicholas and James P. McCubbin, Jr. James P. McCubbin, Sr. may be buried at the Vance-McCubbin cemetery at Eve with other family members, although his grave is not identified by a headstone there.[312]

On June 17, 1825, the widow Mary Polly McCubbin married a neighbor, John Dicken. Earlier, she had applied for a widow's pension based on the services of her husband James P. McCubbin, Sr., but the pension was denied because Polly could present no proof of their marriage other than the family bible. John Dicken, like Polly's first husband, James, was a veteran of the Revolutionary War, having served in battles in Virginia and Kentucky. On March 10, 1853, Polly applied for a pension on the basis of John Dicken's record of military service.[313]

Between 1830 and 1834, some of the children of James P. McCubbin, Sr. and Mary Polly Cook McCubbin emigrated to new settlements in western Illinois, together with members of the Rupe and Bloyd families. At about the same time, other children of James P., Sr., including John and James P., Jr., emigrated to Miller County, Missouri. After a few years in Illinois, sons David and Pleasant McCubbin moved to Benton County, Missouri, near other family members in Miller County. Daughter Eleanor McCubbin and her husband William H. Rupe also had pioneered in Illinois, but in 1839 they deeded the 130 acres which they still owned in Green County, Kentucky, to Eleanor's brother Nicholas McCubbin and in 1839 or in 1840 moved to Johnson County, Missouri.[314]

Although some of the children of James P., Sr. and their families had moved away, Zachariah, his wife, Anne Chism, and their children, and

Nicholas, his wife, Matilda Gumm, and six of their children were living in Green County at the time of the 1850 U. S. Census.[315] A transcription of the McCubbin family bible by Nicholas McCubbin on "sheets of coarse unruled brownish yellowed paper" showed the dates of the birth and death of his father James McCubbin, Sr. and other family members. This document is still in the possession of Thomas Cameron McCubbin, great-grandson of James McCubbin, Sr..[316]

In November, 1853, Mary Polly McCubbin Dicken granted power of attorney to her son Zachariah, probably so he could collect Polly's military pension money for her.[317] Polly died that year in Campbellsville, Kentucky at the age of 89.[318] Some of the members of the McCubbin family continued living in Green County for many generations, and many are still living there today. Gravesites for some forty-two McCubbins who died between 1873 and 1970 have been recorded from the Vance-McCubbin cemetery at Eve in Green County and from other cemeteries in the area. Zachariah and Nicholas, sons of James P. McCubbin, Sr., and Nicholas's wife, Matilda Gumm, are among those buried at the Vance-McCubbin Cemetery. James P. McCubbin, Sr. may also be buried there.[319]

The Vance-McCubbin Cemetery at Eve, Green County, is the final resting place of Nicholas McCubbin (who died in 1869), Zachariah McCubbin (who died 1894) and Nicholas's wife Matilda Gumm (who died 1854), and possibly James P. McCubbin, Sr. (who died in 1824). Other McCubbin descendants are buried here and in other graveyards in the area. (From https://www.graves.com website, with information contributed by Carolyn McCubbins Scott and the photo of the cemetery by CatheaC.)

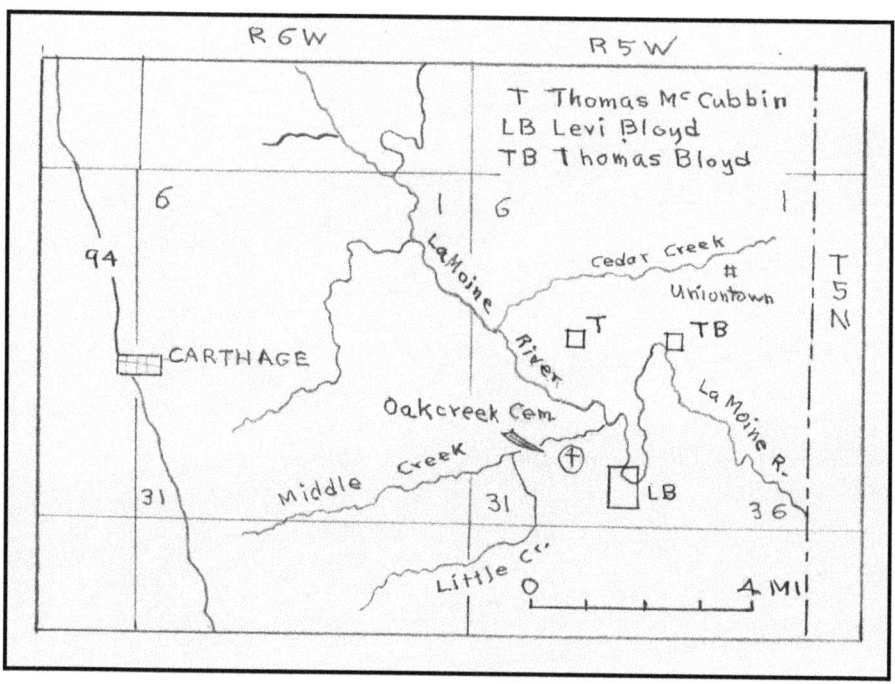

Members of the McCubbin, Bloyd, and Rupe families arrived in Hancock County, Illinois, in 1830 and 1834, and built their log houses on their patented homesteads near "Crooked Creek" (La Moine River on modern maps), about 50 miles west of Beardstown and east of the present town of Carthage. (Patented homesteads from https://www.glorecords.blm.gov.)

Hancock County, Illinois

McCubbin, Bloyd, and Rupe Families

As homestead land opened up farther west, some of the members of the McCubbin family and associated families began moving away from Green County, Kentucky, to western Illinois and Missouri. Hancock County, in western Illinois, was part of an area set aside by Congress to reward veterans of the War of 1812, but settlement was delayed due to hostile Indian activity. Hancock County government was formed in January 1825, Carthage was selected as the county seat, and a log cabin served as the courthouse until 1839. Many new settlers arrived there in the 1830s and 1840s. They established farms to grow their crops and graze their livestock on the virgin prairie, and they filed homestead claims.[320] Today, the area is still a land of farms, small and large, growing mostly corn and soybeans.

A group of McCubbin settlers left Green County, Kentucky, and traveled to Hancock County, Illinois, in 1830, and a second group followed in 1834. The 1830 party, led by Pleasant McCubbin, consisted of at least twenty-nine people, including Pleasant's wife Matilda Rupe and their eight children; Matilda's brother, William H. Rupe and his wife Eleanor McCubbin Rupe; and William and Eleanor's children, aged about 3, 5, and 7.[321] The group also included Levi and Barbara Bloyd and their seven children, John Bloyd, Jr. and his wife, and John Bloyd, Sr. and his wife.[322] The group traveled by oxen-drawn wagon on the old Goshen Road to Sangamon County, near Springfield, where they spent the winter, and then on to southern Hancock County, about fifty miles west of the town of Beardstown, in what is now the Oak Grove School District.[323] They arrived in late September, 1831, when it was late in the season for planting crops.

In a letter written in November 1, 1831, and sent back to family in Green County, Levi and Barbara Bloyd wrote that "we are all tolorable well at this time except Lettle Levi; he has chis [chills] and fevers yet[.] We have all been sick and we got our sickness by going to the Elenoys [Illinois] River," which they crossed before arriving in Hancock County.[324] Levi and Barbara also mention that the corn planted by other settlers that summer was scarce, because it was planted late and had gotten frost-bitten in late September.

Levi and Barbara Bloyd also wrote: "This is fine furtle Coutre[.] We have A plenty of Clard Land and that is good and A plenty of good timber two. A plenty of Stock water, good mill sects [sites?] here[.] We have to dig wells Mostly to use. Best of hog range and all kin of stock But I would Avise purson that come to this plce to Bring all the Cattle they possibly can[.] They are not much expense and they are hard to get here." In this letter, Levi recommended that Nicholas and Zachariah McCubbin move from Green County to this new settlement because "we think they Can do much better here than ther."[325] Despite this advice, Nicholas and Zachariah stayed in Green County, Kentucky.

Levi Bloyd built a log house of two separate buildings connected by a single continuous roof (a style that was common in the pioneer communities). The houses built by Levi and other members of the group were built using pegs and rawhide thongs, as metal nails were not available. Levi's house probably was located on "Crooked Creek" (now the La Moine River) in the east half of section 33, T 5 N, R 5 W, land that he claimed as his homestead in 1840.

Pleasant McCubbin, the leader of the 1830-31 group, built a house just to the northwest of a little ravine, across from the present Oak Grove cemetery.[326] Pleasant was reputed to be an unusually strong man and was famed for the amount of work he could accomplish. He was engaged in freighting with his ox team out of Beardstown, and "No man at either end of his run could compare with him in handling heavy freight. Loading and unloading of barrels of whisky alone was no trick for him."[327] Pleasant also worked for Samuel Brown, helping him build the dam across "Crooked Creek" for his mill run.[328]

In 1832, after their crops were planted, the McCubbin-Rupe-Bloyd group learned of an "Indian scare" in the area, so they moved to Beardstown, about 50 miles to the east, until they felt it was safe to return to their farms.[329] The spring and summer of 1832 was the time of the Blackhawk War, when there were Indian raids on settlers in northern Illinois. After the families returned home to their farms, they learned that the reason for the Indian scare was that "someone had seen a pony track near the settlement."[330] In about 1833, a subscription school was established, and a Baptist minister held church services in the homes of the settlers.[331]

Thomas Bloyd and Elizabeth (McCubbin) Bloyd had arrived in Hancock County in the fall of 1830 with Thomas's uncle, Levi Bloyd, and his wife Barbara. Thomas Bloyd built his house "about one mile north and a quarter of a mile east from where the Bartlett-Huntley-Martin mill was afterwards located."[332] This house probably was on "Crooked Creek" in SW SE section 15, T5N, R5W, land that Thomas claimed in 1840.[333] Thomas brought a small hand mill with him from Kentucky, and "Each family in the settlement used this little mill to grind their bread corn."[334]

A second group of immigrants, including Joseph, Thomas, and David McCubbin, moved with their families from Green County to the settlement in Hancock County in the fall of 1834. Thomas McCubbin built his house on land in SE SE section 17, T5N, R5W, which he claimed in 1840. Joseph built his house about 200 yards to the southwest of where the Oak Grove school house (and perhaps near the present Oak Grove Cemetery) is located. When Joseph built this house, early cold weather made it impossible to keep the mud in a plastic condition while chinking the logs.[335]

Joseph McCubbin and his wife Eleanor Lipsie had arrived in Hancock County with four children, aged 2 to 11, and with Eleanor's father John Lipsey, who had lost a leg while serving in the Revolutionary War.[336] Two children were born to Joseph and Eleanor after they arrived in Hancock County: Turner, who died at age 17, and Thomas Benton, who married Martha Cameron. After the death of his wife, Joseph lived with his son, Thomas, and Thomas's wife Martha, on their homestead.[337]

In the 1830s, several of the families of the McCubbin-Rupe-Bloyd community in Hancock County moved to new land in Missouri.[338] These included the families of Pleasant, Thomas, and David McCubbin and the family of William Rupe and his wife Eleanor McCubbin Rupe, all of whom apparently left Hancock County to join William B. McCubbin and his wife Drusilla Chism in Benton County, Missouri. Other members of the community stayed on in Hancock County, but, in 1857, William W. and Benjamin Bloyd, grandsons of Thomas and Elizabeth Bloyd, joined a wagon train to California. Four years later William W. Bloyd returned to Illinois to lead other members of the Bloyd and Joseph McCubbin families to California, where they eventually settled in Sutter, Shasta, and Tulare Counties. This party included Joseph McCubbin, his son Thomas, and Thomas's wife Martha Cameron McCubbin.

The story of the travel of the Bloyd-McCubbin party across the plains to California, and the history of these families in the San Joaquin Valley, is told by John C. McCubbin, the great-grandson of Joseph McCubbin.[339] The more recent history of the McCubbin family in Reedley County, California, is reported by John C. McCubbin in *The McCubbin Papers, an Early History of Reedley and the 76 Country*.[340]

Osage River Area, Central Missouri

The Osage Indians ceded their lands in Missouri to the U.S. government in 1808 but, for many years, retained the right to hunt in the area. Present-day Miller and Benton Counties, in the northern part of the Ozark Hills in central Missouri, were officially opened up for settlement in 1820.[341] The land shaped by the Osage River and its many tributary streams consists of relatively flat uplands with elevations up to 860 ft., separated by steep-sided valleys and "hollows," with many caves and springs. When the settlers arrived, the uplands were mostly prairie

The Osage River area of Benton County and Miller County was the home of several McCubbin families who arrived independently from Kentucky and Illinois during the 1830s. After the Civil War, one of the McCubbin families moved to a new homestead south of Auglaize Creek, a tributary of the Osage River in Camden County. The valleys of the river and tributary creeks above the dam at Bagnell are flooded by the Lake of the Ozarks.

with scattered stands of oak, hickory, and hazel trees. Wildlife included deer, bears, wolves, cougars, wildcats, and turkeys.[342] The dam at Bagnell, which was completed in 1931, created the Lake of the Ozarks and flooded the valleys of the Osage River and tributary streams, including Auglaize Creek, now the Grand Glaize Arm of the lake. The natural environment is still preserved in areas such as the Patterson Hollow Wild Area in the Lake of the Ozarks State Park.[343]

Early Settlers in Osage River Area

Many of the early settlers in the Osage River area came from Kentucky and Tennessee, having traveled through St. Louis or St. Charles. The settlers generally traveled as family groups, bringing with them all of their possessions. They traveled by wagons, pulled by two or more yokes of oxen, with their household goods, and with their domestic animals following behind. "There were no roads, no railroads, or steamboats. In places there were trails to be followed, but only of the most primitive kind. All of the streams had to be forded, rafted, or crossed by swimming."[344] After arriving, the new settlers had to raise log cabins to shelter their families and to clear the land for planting of their first crops of corn and wheat.

These settlers were family farmers who, with their fields, livestock, and gardens, produced farm products to support themselves and to trade for other necessities at trading centers such as Tuscumbia, a river boat stop on the Osage River. They may have supplemented their diet with game animals from the woods and fish from the nearby streams. Eventually, when roads and other infrastructure were developed, they produced corn, wheat, tobacco, bacon, hams, dried beef, corn whiskey, hides, and furs, which they transported to towns on the Osage River. It was not until the 1850s that locally operated steamboats provided transport to markets in St. Louis and New Orleans.[345]

By 1830, at least sixteen immigrants had settled in present-day Miller County and had obtained federal patents on their homesteads. By the end of 1831, land patents had been recorded for some thirty-six settlers. Among those settlers were Tscharner C. DeGraffenreid, his first wife Elizabeth, and two of their children, William Monroe and

Susan M. DeGraffenreid, who moved to Miller County from Christian County, Kentucky.[346] In 1831, Tscharner was 32 years old, Elizabeth was 29, and William Monroe was 8 years old. The DeGraffenreid family had lived in south-central Virginia during the Revolution, when Tscharner served the American cause and was injured in the battle at Guilford Court House.[347] In 1836, Elizabeth DeGraffenreid joined the Gilgal Baptist Church, the first Baptist Church in the area.[348] In 1837, Tscharner DeGraffenreid was a member of the first petit jury in the Miller County circuit court.[349]

Miller County government was created in 1837, and county justices, a sheriff, and other officers were appointed. The town of Tuscumbia on the Osage River was established as the county seat, and the county was divided into townships to provide administrative services to the scattered settlements.[350] Also, in 1837, a ferry was licensed by the county to provide a crossing of the Osage River at Tuscumbia and was authorized to charge $1.00 for a wagon and two horses, 50 cents for a gig and a horse, and 3 cents each for hogs and sheep.[351]

In the U.S. census of 1840, there were 341 households in Miller County, including that of John McCubbin and his sons William R., Thomas, and Abraham. In Johnson and Benton Counties, the census recorded the households of William B., David B., and Pleasant McCubbin. By the time of the 1850 census, James P. McCubbin, Jr. and his party had arrived and were established in their households in Miller County.

A letter written on June 9, 1859 by an early settler, William L. Irwin, to his brother in Pennsylvania, describes life in the early settlements: "I have saw no part of Mo. that I like as well as where we are. The land here is good. There are rocky ridges of lime stone. It would astonish you to see the grass that grows on these ridges. Horses, mules, cattle, sheep and hogs run in the woods from spring till fall and do well. There is cattle here now fat enough to kill out of the woods. Corn is the principal crop here. It looks well so far. They say we are going to have a better crop of wheat then they have had for some years. Oats look fine . . . There is apples but few peaches in this neighborhood. There will be blackberries by the bushel. They grow on high bushes in vacant places in the woods. Are plenty persimmons and grapes by the wagon load."[352]

McCubbins in Benton County, Missouri

One of the sons of James P. McCubbin, Sr., William B. McCubbin, and William's wife, Drusilla Chism McCubbin, arrived in Benton County, Missouri in the 1830s, apparently directly from Green County, Kentucky. In 1836, William and Drusilla were among the seven founding members of the Spring Grove Baptist Church, meeting in a log school house on Little Tebo Creek, about five miles north of the future site of the town of Warsaw.[353] In the 1850 U. S. census for Benton County, their nine children were 2 to 19 years old. By the time of the 1860 census, Drusilla was the head of household and only Samuel (age 19) and Sarah (age 15) were living with her.[354]

David B. McCubbin, another of the sons of James P. McCubbin, Sr., and David's wife Jane Gumm also arrived in the early 1830s, probably from Hancock County, Illinois. There is no record of them in Benton County until 1847, when David is named as a member of the Spring Grove Baptist Church. In 1860, when land on which the original church building was located was deeded to the church for a new school and "meeting house," David McCubbin was listed as one of the trustees of the church. The log building on Little Tebo Creek was replaced by a new frame building in 1885.[355]

In 1850, David McCubbin lived just a mile east-northeast of the Spring Grove church.[356] He patented his land, totaling 80 acres, in 1854 and 1859 and built a log house on the property. The house was still standing in the 1940s.[357] The 1860 U. S. census shows David, age 45, with his second wife, "Milly" (Amelia Ann Edward), age 38, and nine children in their household. In the 1870 census, David was living with his third wife, Delilah, age 47, and seven children, ages 2 to 23 years.[358] David B. McCubbin, one of the pioneers of Benton County, died in 1908 at the age of about 94 years at the home of his son. David and his wife Amelia are buried in the Kincaid Cemetery, near Warsaw, in Benton County.[359]

Pleasant McCubbin and his wife, the former Matilda Rupe, arrived in Benton County from Hancock County, Illinois, in about 1836.[360] Pleasant built a log house near the site of the later Sterrett homestead west of the future town of Warsaw.[361] He worked as a roustabout on the Osage River steamboats, "often appearing at Tuscumbia in the 1840s."[362] In the 1850 census for Benton County, Matilda McCubbin, age 50, was listed as the head of household and lived with her nine children, ages 5 to 22 years.[363] Pleasant died in 1863 at the age of 59 and is buried at the Kincaid Cemetery near Warsaw, Benton County, Missouri.[364]

Pleasant McCubbin's sister, Eleanor, and her husband, William H. Rupe, sold their 40 acres of land in Green County, Kentucky, to Eleanor's brother Nicholas McCubbin, and in Spring, 1836, they moved from Hancock County, Illinois, to Johnson County, Missouri. In 1844, they sold their property in Johnson County to their two oldest sons, Wesley and Henderson Rupe, and moved to Benton County.[365] In the 1850 U. S. census in Benton County, William H. Rupe, age 46, was living with his wife Ellen (Eleanor) and their six children, ages 4 to 17.[366] William and Eleanor Rupe are buried at the Lewis Roth Cemetery, Warrensburg, Johnson County. Missouri.[367]

Three of the sons of Pleasant and Matilda Rupe McCubbin moved on from Benton County to California. Thomas moved in 1849 and Frank in 1853, and both lived in Marysville, California until their death.[368] A third son, Barnett McCubbin, traveled to California in 1853 and is said to have served on a wagon train as a wagon driver and hunter of wild game. The party arrived in "Hangtown" (Placerville), California, after being on the road for over six months. Barnett reportedly stayed in California for about three and a half years before returning by steamer, crossing the Isthmus of Panama, and arriving in New Orleans. From there he traveled, perhaps by riverboat, to his old home at Warsaw, Missouri.[369]

Sarah (Sally) McCubbin, a daughter of James P. McCubbin, Sr. and Mary Polly Cook, married William Bennight (Bennett?) in Hardin County, Kentucky. Like other members of the McCubbin family, they moved to Miller County, Missouri, in the middle 1830s.[370] William, a miller, practiced his trade at Sarten's Mill (probably a corn meal and flour mill) near the Big Saline Creek, a tributary of the Osage River, and later became the proprietor of the enterprise. William and Sarah left the area in the 1840s, moving to what is now Caldwell County, Missouri.[371]

John McCubbin and the Hawkins/McCubbin Community in Miller County

John McCubbin, the eldest son of James P. McCubbin, Sr. and his wife Elizabeth "Betsy" Lemon, arrived in Miller County from Green County, Kentucky, in the early 1830s with a party of at least fourteen persons, including their ten children, Charity, Nancy, William R., Abraham, Anne, Melvina, Thomas H., Elizabeth, Sarah, and John P.[372] The group evidently also included William R. McCubbin's wife, Nancy Bilyeu, and Abraham's wife, Sarah Dean, and possibly other members of the Bilyeu and Dean families. In 1833, John McCubbin was about 48 years old, Elizabeth was 43, and their children ranged in age from about 2 to 21 years. They evidently settled first in Pulaski County, Missouri, but by 1837 they were in Miller County.

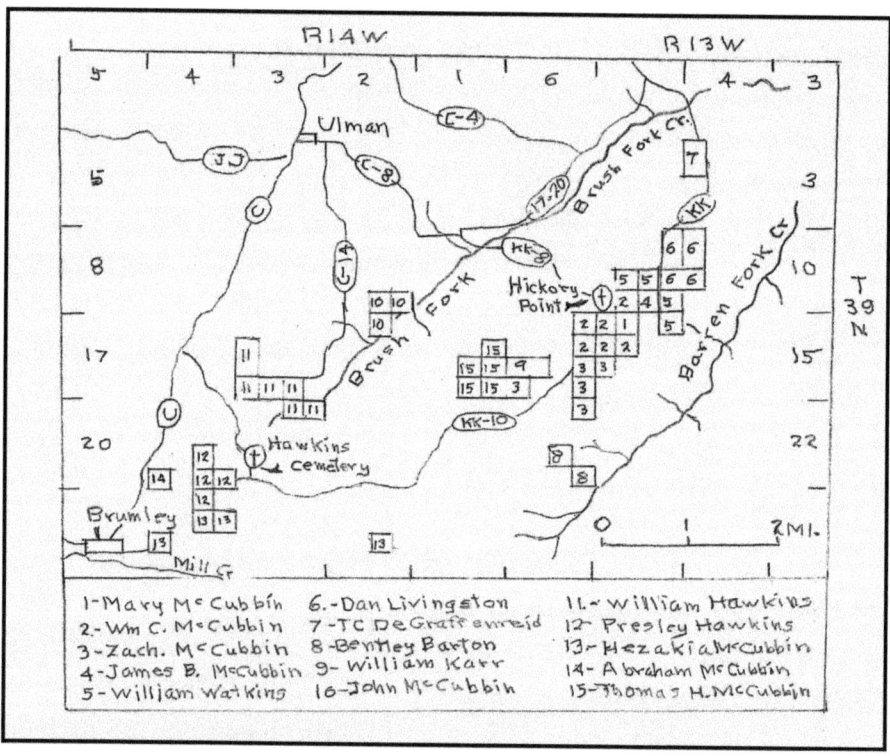

The patented homesteads of the James P. McCubbin, Jr. and John McCubbin families and associated families are centered near the church at Hickory Point between Brushy Fork and Barren Fork Creeks and near the Hawkins Cemetery in the headwaters of Brushy Fork Creek in Miller County. (Land patents from https://www.glorecords.blm.gov.)

When the John McCubbin family arrived in Miller County, they settled on land south of Tuscumbia on Brushy Fork Creek, in what became Glaize Township. In August, 1837, John and three of his sons, William R., Abraham, and Thomas H. McCubbin, petitioned the Miller County Court to establish a new township, Glaize Township, just west of Richwoods Township, and provide a voting place more convenient to their homes south of the Osage River.[373] Their homesteads in Glaize Township were probably the lands they patented starting in 1844.[374]

Many of the roads connecting the scattered settlements were built between 1839 and 1843. William R. McCubbin was a chainman on an 1841 road-survey crew, building the road south from Tuscumbia to Springfield.[375] Also, until 1847, men from ages 18 to 45 were required to muster for military drills and to patrol the roads for horse thieves and other outlaws.[376] In December, 1840, William R. McCubbin observed a reported horse thief, described as "a man with a red beard and two horses," on the road south of Tuscumbia. He joined a muster squad of militia members who followed the horses' tracks and helped capture "red whiskers" at Tuscumbia.[377]

John McCubbin was already established in the area when his brother James P. McCubbin, Jr. arrived in about 1837-38. Most of the members of the James P. McCubbin, Jr. family group started a new community at what became known as Hickory Point in Richwood Township, but James's daughter Catherine and her husband William David Hawkins settled in Glaize Township near the headwaters of Brushy Fork Creek, only a few miles from where John McCubbin and his family were already living. In 1843, Serepta B. McCubbin, another daughter of James P. McCubbin, Jr., married Presley Hawkins and moved to the area in Glaize Township where Catherine and William David Hawkins were living.

William David Hawkins patented his land in 1848-1859, and Presley Hawkins patented his land claims in 1851-1857. By the time of the 1850 census, William and Catherine (McCubbin) Hawkins and their six children, and Presley and Serepta (McCubbin) Hawkins and their two children lived on their land within a three-mile radius of the present Hawkins Cemetery. By the time of the 1860 census, other members of the McCubbin family, including Abraham and Hezekiah McCubbin, sons of John and Elizabeth McCubbin, were living nearby. Willis Burks and his wife Julia Ann McCubbin were living just to the east of the Hawkins settlement. Tscharner (T.C.) DeGraffenreid and his wife Cynthia Ann McCubbin, and their son William Monroe and his wife Elizabeth Ellen McCubbin, lived on land farther west in Glaize Township.[378]

A new mission church was started in the Hawkins/McCubbin community in 1843 by William C. McCubbin, who was by then an ordained minister at the Hickory Point church.[379] In about 1855 this mission church was formally established as the United Baptist Church of Christ. Charter members included Serepta and Presley Hawkins, Catherine and William Hawkins, and seven others.[380] Church meetings were held in homes until sometime before 1859, when a log church was built in the valley of Mill Creek, a tributary of Glaize Creek, and about one-half mile east of the present town of Brumley. The church was by then called the Union Church. Much later, in 1883, a new frame church was built in Brumley, and, in 1891, the name of this successor church was changed to the First Baptist Church at Brumley.[381]

In 1840, Miller County was organized into school districts, and, by 1857, fourteen public school buildings had been built, including one in southwestern Richwood township and another in Glaize Township. William C. McCubbin was a trustee in school district 13, and William Hawkins was a trustee in district 11. In 1847, official listings of the children between the ages of 6 and 20 showed that there were 225 in Richwoods Township and 176 in Glaize.[382] Many of these children, including those of the Hickory Point community, lived miles away from their nearest schoolhouse.

At the time of the 1850 census, John McCubbin, his wife Elizabeth, and three of their children, Thomas H., Elizabeth R., and John P., were living in the Glaize area near the Hawkins community. John McCubbin died in 1860 and Elizabeth died in 1871, and both are buried at the Hawkins Cemetery.[383] By about 1850, two of the other sons of John and Elizabeth, Abraham and William Richmond McCubbin, and William's wife Nancy Bilyeu left the area and traveled west on the Oregon Trail. They claimed land in Clackamus County, east of Oregon City, Oregon.[384] Abraham is buried in Wasco County, west of Oregon City, Oregon. William R. and his wife Nancy Bilyeu McCubbin are buried in the Logan Pleasant View Cemetery, Oregon City.[385] Descendants of William R. and Nancy live in Oregon today.

After the Civil War, some of the members of the Glaize and Richwood communities moved to the new town of Brumley and were active in the Baptist church and in businesses there. Zachariah Taylor (Z. T.) McCubbin, son of William C. and Margaret Watkins McCubbin, served as a member of the board of directors and as a deacon of the First Baptist Church of Brumley (the successor to the Union Church). Early businesses in Brumley included a general store, in a building erected in 1895 by J. M. Hawkins. After the Bagnell dam was completed in 1931 and the Lake of the Ozarks became a sportsman's paradise, a grocery store and service station was established in Brumley by Lloyd and Veda DeGraffenreid.[386]

James P. McCubbin, Jr. and the Hickory Point Community

James P. McCubbin, Jr. and his group of eighteen or more persons arrived in Miller County from Green County, Kentucky, in 1837, probably a short time after James's brother, John had arrived. The new group consisted of James P., Jr., age 48; his wife Mary Parthenia ("Polly") Cook, age 45; and all fourteen of their children, ages 2 years to 25 years. The children were all unmarried except William Cook McCubbin, 25, and his wife, Margaret Canada Watkins, 20, and Catherine McCubbin, 20, and her husband David William Hawkins. During the long, hard journey, the young couples must have helped care for the children in the group. The James P. McCubbin group probably followed the same route as John. They crossed the Osage River at Tuscumbia and traveled south to what became new settlements in the Richwoods and Glaize areas.

James's brother, John, may have helped James and his party select the site where they settled in Richwoods Township, about ten miles south of Tuscumbia along the southwest-trending divide between Brushy Fork Creek and Barren Fork Creek. Miller County Judge Clyde Lee Jenkins wrote that James, after finding a favorable place, "immediately opened the wilderness by clearing a small patch of hickory land. Having stirred the soil enough with a pole plow pulled by a yoke of oxen, James, Mary, and children took several pokes of maize toted in a wagon-box from Kentucky, and planted their first crop. Living first under a crude lean-to constructed of pole and brush, they enjoyed few conveniences, but after dog-days, good weather having assured a bountiful harvest, a large cellar was dug and covered, a smokehouse was erected, and a log dwelling was raised."[387] Supplies that they did not bring with them would have to be obtained from the town of Tuscumbia or by trading with their neighbors.

Between 1853 and 1857, all eleven of the children of James P., Jr. and Mary Polly McCubbin who were unmarried at the time of arrival found spouses among the neighboring families, including the DeGraffenreids, Hawkins, and Burks families. Early marriage services may have been held in the original Hickory Point Baptist Church and were performed by Baptist lay preachers (John Brockman, William Reed, J. M. Brown, and W. B. Karr) and by William C. and Zachariah W. McCubbin, who had become ordained Baptist ministers.[388] Some of the married children of James P., Jr. and Mary Polly McCubbin formed their own separate households and eventually filed their separate claims near the original family farm, establishing the community that became the Hickory Point community. "Now, firmly established, the McCubbin improvement [of James P. McCubbin, Jr. at Hickory Point], with the coming of married sons, and other members of the clan nearby, would become a settlement, and a place for holding social activities, especially church services."[389]

Baptist Church at Hickory Point

The first church in the area was the United Baptist Church of Gilgal, near Bagnell, and early members of that church included Elizabeth DeGraffenreid, who joined in 1836.[390] The church in the Hickory Point area was organized in 1840 by Zachariah W., William, and James P. McCubbin, Jr., along with Reuben Short and William Reed, and called The United Baptist Church of Jesus Christ of Little Richwoods.[391] The ten original members included James P. and Mary McCubbin and their children Zachariah, William, Cynthia Ann, and Serepta.[392] By 1841, membership had increased to fifteen members, and Zachariah W. McCubbin was the preacher. In 1843, Zachariah was officially licensed to preach, and his brother, William C. McCubbin, was ordained to the ministry. This church was officially renamed the Hickory Point Baptist Church, probably in 1845, when the congregation proposed building a new house of worship.³⁹³ This building was evidently replaced in 1873 by another log church building which was the home of the Hickory Point Baptist Church until 1955, when the present church building was completed.³⁹⁴ All of the early log churches were evidently near the present Hickory Point Church and Cemetery, which still serve the surrounding area.

The Hickory Point Baptist Church, shown here, is near the site of the original church founded by the James McCubbin family and others in 1840 and served as the center of the Hickory Point community. This church and cemetery, together with a few nearby houses. are all that remain to mark the location of the community. (Photo by the author.)

The Family of James P. McCubbin, Jr. at Hickory Point

James P. McCubbin, Jr., the patriarch of the Hickory Point community, died in 1841, reportedly of injuries received in an accident.³⁹⁵ At the time of his death, James P., Jr. still owned 140 acres of land in Green County, Kentucky, that he described in his will as "the place that I moved off of when I left that country." His will, written in May 1841, and proved in October, 1841, in Miller County, directs that his land in Green County be sold, that the proceeds be divided among his family, and that his other assets go to his wife, "Polly" (Mary Parthenia), for her use until her death and then to their children. James named his sons William C. and Zachariah W. as executors of his will. James's older brother John McCubbin, who lived nearby in Glaize Township, was one of the witnesses to the will.[396] James P. McCubbin, Jr. was described by Judge Clyde Lee Jenkins, Miller County historian, as "A stern, devout man, and few pioneers contributed more toward development of the area, and the enlightenment of the inhabitants' minds."[397]

In his will, James P. McCubbin, Jr. named his 13 children: William C., Zachariah W., Cynthia Ann, Serepta, Elizabeth, James B., Julia Ann, Emily, Joseph D., John T., Lydia J. B., and Margaret. In the 1850 U. S. census, Mary Parthenia (Polly) McCubbin, then a widow, was head of her household, living with her younger children, Emily N., Margaret, John T., Lydia J. B., and Cynthia Ann (who by then was married to John Snelling). Her son William C. McCubbin lived in his household with his wife, Margaret Watkins, and their five children, ages 1 to 14. Son Zachariah W. McCubbin lived nearby with his wife, Susannah M. DeGraffenreid and their children, Pernicia, Louis C., and William. Daughter Julia Ann was married to Willis Burks and was living with her husband's parents.[398] By the time of the 1860 census, Elizabeth McCubbin had married William Monroe DeGraffenreid and was living in the Glaize area.

In 1848, McCubbin family members began patenting the lands where they lived in the settlement near the Hickory Point Church. Mary Parthena McCubbin, the widow of James P., Jr., claimed the 40 acres where she lived with her younger children in March 1848. William C. McCubbin patented his six 40-acre plots adjacent to his mother's land between 1848 and 1860. Zachariah W. McCubbin claimed three 40-acre plots just south of his mother between 1849 and 1865, and James B. McCubbin patented a 40-acre plot nearby in 1851. Thomas H. and John P. McCubbin, sons of John and Elizabeth, also patented 40-acre plots nearby to the southwest in 1859 and 1860.[399] Thus, three of the sons of James P. McCubbin, Jr. and two of the sons of James's brother John had secured about 640 acres of land within a two-mile radius of the Hickory Point Church. William Karr, Daniel Livingston, William Watkins, and Bentley Barton, whose daughters married into these McCubbin families, also patented 40-acre plots adjacent to the McCubbin lands and were part of the Hickory Point community.[400]

William C. McCubbin and his wife Margaret Canada Watkins, who were part of the family group that made up the Hickory Point community, had eight children, born between 1835 and 1861. Three of these children married other members of the Hickory Point community: Mary E. married John T. Livingston, James Albert married Mary Frances Barton, and Zachariah T. married Eliza McCombs.[401] William C. McCubbin was still living at Hickory Point during the Civil War, when he served in the Missouri State Guard. He and his wife Margaret are buried in the Livingston Cemetery, about two miles east of Hickory Point.[402]

Zachariah W. McCubbin married Susannah DeGraffenreid, daughter of Tscharner C. DeGraffenreid and his first wife, Elizabeth, on December 24, 1844, after they arrived in Miller County. Their wedding was performed by J. Brockman, another very early settler.[403] Zachariah, along with other family members, was one of the founders, in 1840, of the original Baptist church at Hickory Point and, in 1841, he was licensed to preach at that church.[404] He was later, on September 5, 1845, elected Clerk and Treasurer of the Miller County Association of Baptist Churches.[405] Zachariah, like his brother William C., officiated at many weddings in the years before the Civil War.[406]

Zachariah's six children were born at Hickory Point between 1847 and 1855. Zachariah died on September 24, 1855, at the age of 41, of causes unknown, at Hickory Point, Richwoods Township. His wife, Susannah, was only 28 years old at the time. Their children were also quite young. Pernicia was 8, Lewis C. was 7, William was 5, Mary F. was 4, Parthenia was 2, and Louisa B. was a newborn baby. By the time of the 1860 U. S. Census, five of the children were still living in their Hickory Point home with their mother, Susannah, together with Ellen K. DeGraffenreid, who then was 22 years old.

In 1864, Susannah's daughter, Pernicia, married Robert Kirkpatrick Jeffries; in 1868, Louis C. married Jemimah Barton; in 1873, Mary F. married Louis Castleman; in 1877, Parthenia married James B. Watkins; and in 1875, Louisa married John Pennington.[407] Thus, by 1877 all of Susannah's children had married other members of the Hickory Point community and had moved out of the McCubbin household. By the time of the 1880 census, Susannah was living with her daughter Louisa and Louisa's husband John Pennington and their young children in Glaize Township, Miller County.

Other Early Families at Hickory Point

As mentioned before, Tscharner C. DeGraffenreid and his family arrived in Miller County from Christian County, Kentucky sometime before June 22, 1837. They may have settled first about two miles north of Hickory Point on land that Tscharner patented in 1848.[408] Tscharner's son William Monroe DeGraffenreid married Elizabeth Ellen McCubbin on April 2, 1844, and Zachariah McCubbin performed the wedding ceremony. Tscharner's daughter Susannah M. DeGraffenried married Zachariah W. McCubbin on December 24, 1844. Then, on March 9, 1858, Tscharner himself married Cynthia Ann McCubbin, as his second wife. John Brockman performed the service.[409] By the time of the 1860 census, members of the DeGraffenreid family had moved to Glaize Township and, after the Civil War, to a new community near the Miller County-Camden County border, where Lewis McCubbin and his wife Jemimah Barton had settled.

Bentley A. Barton and his wife Elizabeth A. Hendon came from Graves County, Kentucky, in about 1857-1858 with six of their children. Two of the daughters who arrived with them married McCubbin sons: Mary Francis Barton married James A. McCubbin, son of William McCubbin and Margaret Watkins, in 1867, and Jemimah Catherine Barton married Lewis C. McCubbin in 1868. The other seven Barton children were born after they arrived in Richwood Township.[410] The Bartons patented two 40-acre homesteads, about a mile south of the McCubbin lands, in April and June, 1860.[411] After the Civil War, when many left the community, Bentley Barton and his wife Elizabeth were among the few who continued living in the Hickory Point area. They are buried at the Hickory Point Cemetery, ant their daughter Mary Frances Barton and her husband James A. McCubbin are also buried at Hickory Point.[412]

Daniel and Parthena Livingston arrived from Hart County, Kentucky, in about 1854 and patented land at Hickory Point in 1857-1860.[413] Shortly after arriving they joined the Hickory Point Baptist Church and were prominent members for the rest of their lives. One of their sons, John T. Livingston, married Mary E. McCubbin, daughter of William C. and Margaret McCubbin, in 1858. Another son,

Richard V. Livingston married Emily F. McCubbin in 1867. Both of these weddings were performed by William C. McCubbin.[414] After the death of Daniel Livingston in 1864, John T. and Mary E. Livingston took over the family homestead at Hickory Point, adding that to the land they had patented in 1859-1860. Mary E. (McCubbin) Livingston had been an active member of the Hickory Point Church for eighty-one years at the time of her death in 1932. She is buried at the Livingston Cemetery east of Hickory Point.[415]

Olive Waite Livingston, granddaughter of Daniel and Parthenia Livingston, wrote about life in the Hickory Point community after the Civil War era, based on family documents and stories and on childhood memories of her visits there.[416] She describes how the families grew their own food and obtained other supplies they needed in the town of Tuscumbia. Fruits and vegetables were grown in their own orchards and gardens. A hog and, occasionally a beef, were butchered in the fall with the help of neighbors. Meat was smoked or preserved in brine. There were always some chickens for eggs and for a pot of chicken and dumplings now and then. Once or twice a year a load of corn or wheat was taken to a mill to be ground. There was always a cane patch, and homemade molasses was the only sweetener. Many settlers spun wool from their own sheep to knit and weave clothing and blankets.

Another settler at Hickory Point, William S. Watkins, had been persuaded to settle there by his aunt, Margaret Canada Watkins, wife of William C. McCubbin, after he returned from the California gold rush.[417] In 1855 William Watkins married Mary Jane Livingston, and, in 1857-1860, he patented land on the east and north sides of the Hickory Point community.[418] His daughter Lucy S. Watkins married Thomas H. McCubbin, son of John and Elizabeth McCubbin of Glaize Township, in 1857, and the couple apparently settled at Hickory Point.[419] During the Civil War, William S Watkins served in the Missouri State Guard and, according to one story, was killed in a skirmish with a federal army unit in southern Camden County when he fell from his horse and was shot by a Union soldier.[420] His body was brought back home, buried in a field on his farm, and later moved to the Hickory Point Cemetery.[421]

McCubbins During the Civil War

Although Missouri was admitted to the Union as a slave-holding state, the number of slave owners in Miller County was never very large. Sixty-nine slave owners were listed in the assessor's book for Miller County in 1859, and none of the slave owners in the assessor's book or in the census records were McCubbins or other residents of the Hickory Point or Hawkins communities.[422] Residents who came from states such as Virginia, North Carolina. and Kentucky generally had sympathies for the principle of state's rights and for the Confederacy. Former residents of northern states and recent immigrants who had no connection to any particular state supported the Union. It is estimated that, during the Civil War, about 300 residents of Miller County supported the Confederacy and nearly 700 upheld the Union in militia or regular troops.[423]

Judge Clyde Lee Jenkins, who wrote about the history of the Civil War in Miller County, noted that "Events leading directly to Civil War in Miller County commenced in January,1861. Huge mass meetings were held at Tuscumbia, Iberia, Ulman's Ridge, and Pleasant Mount. At these meetings the citizens of Miller County discussed Governor Claiborn Fox Jackson's call for a state constitutional convention. Since a question on secession was involved, the election of delegates to this state convention was soon the bitterest and most heated subject in the discussion of the inhabitants."[424] In March, 1861, Governor Jackson declared his desire to secede from the Union, and in April he called up Missouri State Guard units "for maneuvers" at Camp Jackson in St. Louis. On May 10, Captain National Lyon, commander of the Union forces in St. Louis, captured the State Guard troops and fired upon civilian protesters, killing fifteen persons and wounding many others.[425]

In Miller County, after the events at Camp Jackson in May, several volunteer units were organized by local leaders to support the governor and to defend the county against Lyon's federal troops. One of these State Guard units was formed in Richwood Township, with William C. McCubbin as Captain.[426] In May, this group assembled near the Hickory Point Church and received two wagon loads of powder and shot from the governor. The guard unit was divided into two smaller groups to sweep through Richwood and Glaize Townships and "ascertain the loyalties of certain families". According to Judge Jenkins, they were confronted in Glaize Township by a group of well-armed men including William Hawkins, husband of Catherine McCubbin, who reportedly "told Captain McCubbin to quit tormenting the local citizenry, . . . and the opposing parties separated, departing peaceably."[427]

In May, 1861, several Home Guard units, supported by the provisional state government installed by the U. S. Army, were organized in Miller County to resist the "secesh" groups and to support the Union. Elected officers of these units included William Hawkins, 1st lieutenant of Company D, and Emly Golden who was elected colonel of the combined forces. A camp, "Fort Union," was established on Mill Creek in Glaize Township.[428] On June 14, one of those units, led by Colonel Emly Golden, ambushed Captain McCubbin's State Guard men in Richwood Township and scattered them without a fight. The next morning, the remnants of the State Guard company, intending to travel to Jefferson City to join General Price there, returned home when they were told by the ferryman at Tuscumbia that the federals were already in the capital and on all the roads leading to the capital.[429] On June 25, Colonel Golden's forces captured and occupied the courthouse at Tuscumbia.[430]

In August, 1861, Confederate General Sterling Price moved north from Springfield routing Union forces and, in September, defeated Union troops at Lexington. Stirred by these Confederate successes, remnants of the State Guard companies in Richwood Township evidently renewed their harassment of Union supporters. In the afternoon of September 25, 1861, men rode up to the house of William Hawkins in Glaize Township, and Catherine (McCubbin) Hawkins, William's wife, watched the men "lead the big mare and the little bay mare away; carrying from the house, smokehouse, and log stable other sundries."[431]

The second phase of the war in Miller County began with the organization of volunteers "for the term of three years or during the war" and the formation of state militias armed and equipped by the U. S government. William Hawkins, 1st Lieutenant of Company D, and other officers took their boys into the U. S. army's 6th Cavalry, Missouri Volunteers. On September 14, 1862, William Hawkins was shot and killed in action at Helena, Arkansas.[432] Also in 1862, Abraham McCubbin, a son of Nicholas McCubbin and Matilda Gumm, was killed in the battle at Lone Jack, near the southeast edge of present-day Kansas City. He was a member of the U. S. 8th Missouri Cavalry and was one of seventy-seven Union soldiers killed at Lone Jack, according to a monument at the site.[433] William C. McCubbin, who led a state militia group supporting the Confederacy early in the war, later served in Company E., 48th Regiment, Confederate Army and died in the regimental hospital in Rolla, Missouri, on November 11, 1864. He is buried at the Livingston Cemetery, two miles east of Hickory Point.[434]

Hickory Point (Watkins) After the Civil War

When hostilities ceased, Miller County was a place of "divided families, many political factions, and community rivalries."[435] Under the new state constitution, anyone who was a "southern sympathizer in any particular" was denied the right to vote, to hold public office, or to practice as a lawyer, a clergyman, or a teacher unless he had subscribed to "The Iron Oath" of loyalty. Hezekiah McCubbin, son of William C. McCubbin, was an early southern sympathizer who later entered the service of the United States and was honorably discharged. Because he had been a southern sympathizer, Hezekiah lost his right to vote but successfully petitioned to have his rights restored.[436] Among the many other cases of legal and civil action against Southern supporters who survived the war, no other McCubbin is named.[437]

During the years 1864 and 1865, the Hickory Point Church was temporarily closed "because all male members were in the United States service."[438] As mentioned earlier, William C. McCubbin, husband of Margaret Canada Watkins, served in State Guard and, later, in the Confederate Army and died in a prisoner-of-war camp in Rolla, Missouri. William Watkins, while serving in the Missouri State Guard, was shot and killed in a skirmish in Miller County and was brought home for burial. Bentley Barton served in Company E, 3rd Regiment, Missouri Cavalry, Confederate Army, and returned home to his family after the war. William McCubbin's son, William H. McCubbin, served in Company E, 48th Missouri Infantry,[439] and his son Hezekiah served first in the State Guard and later in the Union Army.[440] Some of the other members of the Hickory Point community, including three of the sons of Daniel Livingston and also the son of David Castleman, served in the Union Army.[441]

These old farm buildings, behind a more recent house, are immediately south of the Hickory Point Church and Cemetery, on land patented by William C. McCubbin. On a 1904 plat of the area, these buildings are shown as the property of Silas P. McCubbin, youngest son of William C. and Margaret Watkins McCubbin. (Photo by the author, June 2002.)

After the war, the Watkins, Livingston, and Barton families became the predominant families of the community.[442] By 1904, J. B. Watkins operated a general store in the community, then called "Watkins," which also had a post office and a school. Silas P. McCubbin and James Albert McCubbin, sons of William C. McCubbin, were the only members of the McCubbin family still living at Hickory Point.[442] The 1904 plat shows three buildings directly south of the Hickory Point Church, on land owned by S. (Silas) P. McCubbin.[443] Today, an old house and barn located just south of Hickory Point Church may be two of the buildings shown on the 1904 plat and may be the oldest surviving remnants of the early Hickory Point community. The general store and other buildings of

Watkins are also gone. The Hickory Point Baptist Church and Cemetery and a few houses are all that remain from the Hickory Point community. Of the descendants of the early McCubbin members of the community, only James Albert McCubbin, husband of Mary Francis Barton, and Silas P. McCubbin and his three wives are known to be buried at the Hickory Point Cemetery.[444]

On March 22, 1868, when living with his widowed mother, Susannah, in Hickory Point, Lewis McCubbin married his neighbor Jemimah Catherine Barton and soon thereafter moved to a new homestead in Camden County, Missouri.[445] Lewis was then almost twenty years old, and Jemimah, the daughter of Bentley Barton and Elizabeth Ann Hendon, was seventeen.[446] Lewis's mother Susannah continued living at Hickory Point/Watkins but, by the time of the 1880 U. S. Census, was living with her daughter Louisa Pennington in Glaize Township, Miller County.

Camden County, Missouri

Camden County was established in 1841, but it was not until 1855 that the town of Linn Creek was selected to be the county seat. Settlements near the Auglaize Creek, a major tributary of the Osage River, were among the earliest settlements in Camden County, perhaps because they were close to the established settlements in Richwood and Glaize Townships of western Miller County and the supply center of Tuscumbia on the Osage River. When Lewis and Jemimah McCubbin moved to the Auglaize area, there evidently were other settlers in the area north and east of Auglaize Creek along the border between Camden and Miller Counties.

Early Settlers on the Auglaize Creek

The first settlers in the Auglaize area may have been the Jeffries and Huddleston families, who homesteaded on the north and east sides of Auglaize Creek. The Jeffries family patented 40-acre plots starting in 1849 in the southwest quarter of section 28, T19N, R15W, and the Huddlestons patented 40-acre plots in the southeast quarter of section 33, T19N, R15W in 1851.[447] In the area directly north of Auglaize Creek, near the future town of Kaiser, the first family to patent land may have been that of William Monroe DeGraffenreid in 1878, but Tscharner DeGraffenreid and other members of the DeGraffenreid family followed in the 1880s and 1890s.[448]

It is likely that Lewis and Jemimah McCubbin were the first to settle in the area south of Auglaize Creek, where they were connected to the neighbors farther north by a natural ford across the creek. They probably

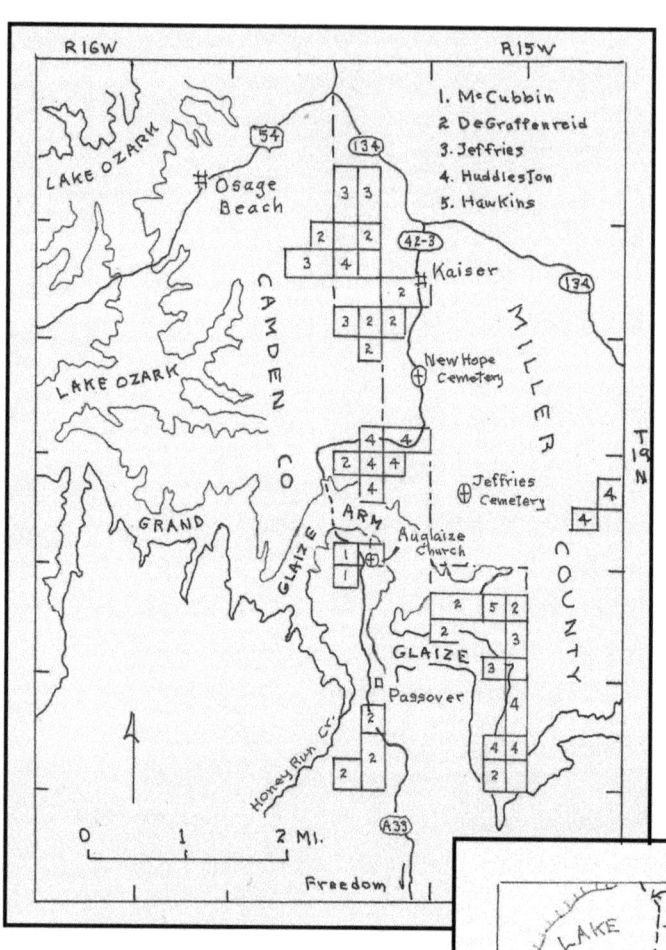

The earliest settlers in the area of Miller and Camden Counties to the north and east of Auglaize Creek (now Grand Glaize arm of the Lake of the Ozarks) were the Huddlestons, Jeffries, and DeGraffenreids, whose patents were recorded beginning in 1849. (Land patents from https://www.glorecords.blm.gov.)

Lewis and Jemimah McCubbin established their homestead south of a ford across Auglaize Creek in Camden County in about 1868 on the land that they patented in 1892. The farm where they and their family lived until about 1930 is now McCubbin Point in Lake of the Ozarks State Park. (Land patents from https://www.glorecords.blm.gov.

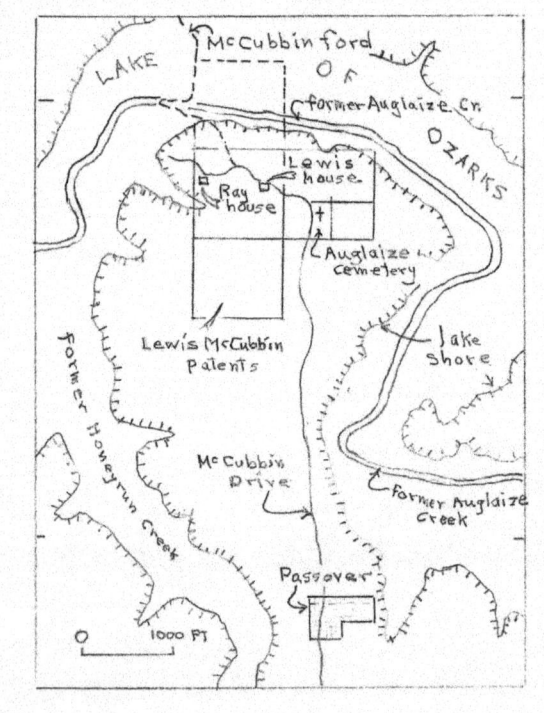

arrived on their land there in the summer or fall of 1868 but did not patent their land until November 11, 1892.[449] Neighbors immediately to the south of the McCubbins may have included the Foxens, who patented land in 1888 and 1904, and the Blankenships, who patented land in 1888 and 1905.[450] Farther south, near the town of Passover, the neighbors of the McCubbins included Tscharner DeGraffenreid and other members of the DeGraffenreid family by 1892. John King DeGraffenreid patented land there in 1893, and William Monroe and his wife Elizabeth Ellen McCubbin DeGraffenreid patented their land in the Passover area by 1904.[451]

For these settlers, both north and south of Auglaize Creek, the town of Zebra (now part of Osage Beach) may have been a supply center at least as early as 1886. Zebra was not established as a town with a store and post office until about 1886 but may have been a riverboat stop much earlier.[452] One source reports that William Jeffries had a blacksmith shop in Zebra, and Frank Anderson kept the Zebra Hotel there and ferried people across the Osage River. On a Rand McNalley map of Camden County published in 1910, the distance to Zebra may have been as little 3 miles on the Zebra-Passover road, crossing McCubbin ford on Auglaize Creek. The distance on modern county road 42-3 through Kaiser to the former town of Zebra is about 5.5 miles.

The McCubbin Farmhouse

After arriving south of Auglaize Creek in about 1868, Lewis and Jemimah built the log cabin where all of their children were born. The first child, Mary E. McCubbin, must have been born in 1868, shortly after they arrived. Their second child, Zachariah M., was born on February 2, 1871; James O. (Ollie) McCubbin was born on October 10, 1872 (or 1873); Miranda Jane (Janie) on March 17, 1880 (or 1882); Carl Bruell on December 18, 1883; and Ray on April 19, 1888.[453] It was not until about 1892 that Lewis and Jemimah built the clapboard house where they lived until 1930, when they moved to Linn Creek. Ray, after he was married in 1917, built a house for his family just northwest of his father's house.

The original log cabin and clapboard house are shown in a photo made in about 1930 by Letisha McCubbin, Ray McCubbin's wife.

Another photo, probably taken at about the same time, shows Lewis and Jemimah McCubbin seated near the door of their house. The stone wall which separated the house from the Zebra-Passover road, which ran along the front or southwest side of the house, and a few other stone relicts are almost hidden in the grass and brush on the southwest side of the present road, McCubbin Drive. The Lewis and Ray McCubbin houses were located near the sign which marks the McCubbin Point Recreation site, a camping and boat launch facility in Lake of the Ozarks State Park.[454]

The log cabin, on the left in this photo, was built by Lewis and Jemimah McCubbin when they arrived in the area, and the clapboard farmhouse probably was built in about 1892 when Lewis patented his homestead. Remnants of the original stone wall or fence on the front of the house near the old road are almost hidden in the grass and brush today. (This photo, made in 1930 by Ray McCubbin's wife Letisa, is from the files of Suellen McCubbin White.)

Lewis and Jemimah McCubbin, in this photo, are seated by door of their farmhouse on Auglaize Creek near Passover, now McCubbin Point. (Photo by Leticia McCubbin, Ray's wife, probably in the late 1920s. From the files of Suellen McCubbin White.)

The Auglaize Church

Before the construction of the first church in the Auglaize area, the McCubbins and their neighbors may have held church services in their homes or perhaps travelled to Zebra. A photo taken in 1907 (according to writing on the back) shows Ray, Bruell, and friends at the cliffs near Zebra, where they may have been attending church services. On February 6,1894, Lewis McCubbin deeded 12 acres of his land (in the southwest quarter of section 20, T19N, R15W) to the church trustees, W. C. Jeffries, Z. M. DeGraffenreid, and T. C. DeGraffenreid, to provide the site for a new church, to be called the Auglaize Baptist Church [455] It is not known when the church was built and the associated cemetery was established, but on February 18, 1919, the trustees, W. M. Woolsey, J. B. DeGraffenreid, and W. C. Jeffries, deeded eight acres back to Lewis, retaining four acres where the church and cemetery were located.[456]

The Auglaize Cemetery monument on the side of the road at McCubbin Point marks the site of the Auglaize Church and Cemetery, now almost hidden in the brush. The names of Tscharner C. DeGraffenreid, his wife Cynthia McCubbin, William Monroe DeGraffenreid, and his wife Elizabeth Ellen McCubbin are among those listed on the monument. (The photo was provided by Etta Jane Hays to Donald McCubbin in October 2005.)

According to local historian Clara Snapp: "The original Auglaize Church was a rough sawn lumber building about 20 ft. x 30 ft. It had a double front door and a single back door. The hearthstone was from the nearby creek." She stated that "the DeGraffenreids started it and Lewis McCubbin was the preacher." According to Clara, the church was located about 500 ft north and west of the Auglaize Cemetery and east of the old Passover-Zebra road.[457] No traces of the original Auglaize church building have been found.

The Auglaize Cemetery, now almost hidden in the brush, was resurveyed in 2004 by the Missouri Department of Natural Resources, and a stone monument for the cemetery was placed on the present road near the cemetery in 2005 by members of the DeGraffenreid and McCubbin families.[458] The Auglaize Cemetery monument includes the names of Tscharner C. DeGraffenreid and his wife Cynthia McCubbin, William Monroe DeGraffenreid and his wife Elizabeth Ellen McCubbin, and other members of the DeGraffenreid, Jeffries, and Snelling families.[459]

Family of Lewis and Jemimah McCubbin

Mary E. (Mollie) McCubbin, the first-born child of Lewis and Jemimah, married James David Shipman on February 25, 1886, and died on August 15 (or September 1), 1888, at the age of about 20. Mary and James David had a son, Celestial Braston (C. B.) Shipman, and another son, William R. Shipman, who lived only a few months.[460] When Mary

This photo of family and friends was "Taken at Zebra, Missouri, the third Sunday in February, 1907. We're standing at a cliff at the mouth of the Glaize [Auglaize Creek]," as recorded on the back of the photo. Persons identified on the photo include: in the back, from the left, Ray McCubbin, age 19, and C. B. (Bruell) McCubbin, 24. (From family sources.)

died, her son C. B., who was then only about 2 years old, went to live with his grandmother and grandfather, Jemimah and Lewis McCubbin, until James David remarried in January, 1890. During their short time together, Mary and her husband James David Shipman lived on a farm near his father's place at Honeyrun, near Passover. C. B. married Ellen Avorine Byrd, and they had eight children together. C. B. lived to celebrate his 100th birthday.[461]

Janie McCubbin married Ed Turpin, a former classmate at the Passover school. Janie died on March 17, 1906, at the age of 24, probably in childbirth. She was buried, with her baby daughter (according to local resident Hadley Shipman), behind the McCubbin farm house, near the present road.[462] The gravesite was surrounded by a rectangular rock wall, part of which is still standing, as pointed out by family historian Clara Snapp and observed by Donald McCubbin when he visited there. (Note that the death and burial of both Mary and Janie may have been before the founding of the cemetery near the Auglaize Church.)

Zachariah (Z. M. or Zach) McCubbin married Ella Nora DeGraffenreid on March 18, 1909, at the age of about 38 years. Ella Nora was the daughter of John King DeGraffenreid and Mary Emiline Morris and was the granddaughter of William Monroe DeGraffenreid. In 1912, Z. M. and Ella Nora moved to Henryetta, Oklahoma, living at 1105 W. Trudgeon Street.[463] Z. M. worked as a carpenter in Henryetta and was a member of the carpenters' union for over 50 years. Z. M. and Ella Nora had three children, Sybil, Joel, and Elson. Ella Nora died on June 29, 1961, at her home on Trudgeon St. and was buried at West Lawn Cemetery in Henryetta, Oklahoma.[464] Zachariah (Z. M.) McCubbin died on March 5, 1963, at the age of 92 years, at the home of his daughter and son-in-law, Sybil and Ben Watkins, in Xenia, Ohio. A death notice for Zachariah was published in the Henryetta *Free Lance* newspaper. He is buried at the Valley View Memorial Gardens, Xenia, Ohio.[465]

Carl Bruell McCubbin (C. B. or Bruell) married Bernice Ray Wilson on July 12, 1908 at the home of his father, Lewis McCubbin. The wedding was officiated by J. W. Jeffries, Minister of the Gospel. Witnesses were James S. Huddleston, J. W. Jeffries, and W. S. Boyd. Bernice was only 17 years old and was married with her parent's consent.[466] Family legend has it that Bernice worked in the McCubbin household before she and

Bruell were married. She was the daughter of Fred Wilson and Julia Anne McCommons. Fred Wilson was born in Germany and moved to Missouri with his parents in about 1861. He married Julia Anne in 1879 and raised a family of 10 children, probably in Hannibal, Missouri, where Bernice was born on February 19, 1891.[467] Children born of the marriage of Bruell McCubbin and Bernice Wilson include Edman Gale McCubbin, born on June 23, 1909, Gladys Pauline on January 14,1913, Thelma Mildred on August 5,1915, and Glenn Omer on October 7, 1921, all in Camden County,[468] Doyle Wayne was born on September 30, 1931, after the family moved to Oklahoma.[469]

James Oliver "Ollie" McCubbin may have married, first, according to unconfirmed reports, Eliza May Schooley on November 20, 1902. He married Alta Pearl Jeffries on December 17, 1916, in Kaiser, Miller County. Alta was the daughter of Derrick W. Jeffries and Mary Emaline Huddleson and was the granddaughter of Pernicia H. McCubbin (Lewis C. McCubbin's sister) and Robert Kirkpatrick Jeffries. Ollie and Alta were the parents of three children: Jewell, Burnell, and Buell. At the time of the 1920 census, Ollie, Alta, Jewell and Buell were living in the farm home of Lewis and Jemimah. Ollie later lived in Eldon, Missouri and died there on June 28, 1952.[470] Alta died September 28, 1977, in Jefferson City, Missouri.[471] Both Ollie and Alta are buried at the New Hope Baptist Church Cemetery near Kaiser, together with other members of the Jeffries and Huddleston families.[472] Pernicia McCubbin and her husband Robert K. Jeffries are buried in the Jeffries family cemetery, north of the Auglaize in Miller County.[473]

Ray McCubbin married Laura Leticia ("Tish") McCulley on December 23, 1917. Leticia was the daughter of William Howell McCulley and Elizabeth Fudge.[474] Ray worked as a farm hand on the Moulder farm, which adjoined the McCubbin property on the south and west. A photo shows Ray McCubbin and Buck and Benny Moulder watering their horses at McCubbin's Ford on Auglaize Creek.[475] Ray probably also helped with the work on the McCubbin farm (by this time, Lewis was 68 years old and Jemima was 65). Ray and Leticia had two children. Their first son, Carroll, was born March 17, 1919, and died March 19, 1919. Their second son, James Merrill, was born on June 17, 1920.[476] Both children were born at Ray and Leticia's house just north and west of the Lewis McCubbin farmhouse. The 1920 U. S. Census for Camden County shows Lewis, Catherine (Jemimah), and also James O. (Ollie) and Alta and two of their young children, living in the McCubbin household.

An article in the Linn Creek newspaper, *The Reveille*, reported that, in the summer of 1922, Ray and some friends caught a 50-pound catfish, barehanded, at or near the same spot where Lewis McCubbin and George W. Salsman had caught two catfish weighing 50 and 51 pounds some forty years earlier. Another item in *The Reveille* reported that Mr. and Mrs. Ray McCubbin and Mr. and Mrs. John Fudge (probably Mrs. McCubbin's sister and brother-in-law) visited friends in Linn Creek on Sunday, February 6, 1925.[477] Some sources say that Ray and Leticia were separated or perhaps divorced in the 1930s, perhaps when the McCubbin farm was sold and Ray moved to Linn Creek. Letisha died May 18, 1987 in Richland, Missouri.[478]

Passover and the Passover School

The little town of Passover and the Passover school are generally considered to have been founded by John King DeGraffenreid, one of the sons of William Monroe DeGraffenreid and his wife Elizabeth Ellen McCubbin. The one-room log school in Passover had its beginning by 1883, on land owned by John King DeGraffenreid, before he transferred

The Passover school house, shown here, is said to be the oldest log school building in Camden County and is still standing in its original location in the town of Passover. (Photo by the author, June 2002.)

The Passover baseball team, shown here, played on the area that is still an open field on the west side of McCubbin Drive near Passover. Ray McCubbin is on the far left, Zach is fourth from the left, and C. B. (Bruell) McCubbin is on the far right. (Photo from Clara Snapp and family sources.)

Students of Passover School, class of 1927/28, in this photo include Meryl "Mac" McCubbin, in the front row, 5th from the left, kneeling. Others include members of the DeGraffenreid, Salsman, and Jeffries families. (This photo, from family sources, was also published in Linn Creek(?) newspaper, newspaper clipping, date unknown.)

title in 1886. The school building was in continuous use until the final year of classes in 1940 and is said to be one of oldest log schools still standing in Camden County. The alumni of the Passover school gathered for reunions there for many years.[479]

School records transcribed by Clara Snapp show that Mary, Zachariah, and James O. McCubbin were students at the Passover school starting in 1883, and Ray, Bruell, and Jane were attending there by 1893.[480] When they were teenagers, Zach, Bruell, and Ray played baseball with the Passover team at the ball diamond, still an open field just north of Passover on the west side of McCubbin Drive. A photo shows them in their baseball uniforms. Another photo shows Bruell and his brothers working as part of a county road crew on a road down to Lyles Crossing on the Auglaize near the McCubbin farm.[481]

The Passover Baptist Church was built in about 1919-1921, even though the old Auglaize Church was just a short distance away. John King DeGraffenreid, John B. DeGraffenreid, and Lewis McCubbin were among those who served as aldermen of the Passover church.[482] A general merchandise store was started in Passover in about 1921 by Jim and Sade DeGraffenreid. They later sold the building and the store merchandise to the Moulder, Salsman, and Vincent families, who operated the store until about 1930. By this time, the nearby farmland had been sold to the developers of the Bagnold dam, that formed the Lake of the Ozarks, and many of the local residents had moved away. Later, after the surrounding land became part of the Lake of the Ozarks State Park, the Stampers and Snellings took over some of the old properties in Passover to sell supplies to fishermen and boaters passing through the town to McCubbin Point.[483]

Tscharner (T. C.) DeGraffenreid and his wife may have lived with their son William Monroe DeGraffenreid or with one of their grandsons in the Passover area because there is no record that he patented land there. T. C. evidently had a reputation as a rifleman and hunter. J. W. Vincent, who lived at Passover and owned a store there, reported that on a Christmas day, when T. C. and his wife had no provisions to feed the family, T.C. took his rifle in hand, with the only two bullets in his possession, and shot a wild turkey "out of the air" to provide a feast for his family.[484] T.C. DeGraffenreid died in 1880 at the age of 81 and is buried at the Auglaize Cemetery. His son William Monroe and William's wife Elizabeth Ellen McCubbin are also buried at the Auglaize Cemetery.[485]

McCubbin Family in Linn Creek

When construction of the Bagnell Dam was begun in 1929, the McCubbin farm and other properties in the area were bought by the Union Electric Land and Development Company.[486] The land was later deeded to the U. S. government[487] and then to the State of Missouri, becoming part of the new Lake of the Ozarks State Park.[488] After the sale of their farm, Lewis and Jemimah, who were then 85 and 82 years old, moved to the new town of Linn Creek, which was established when "old" Linn Creek was flooded by the new lake. They lived in the former two-story brick schoolhouse, built in 1895 in Linn Creek and occupied today by the Camden County Museum.[489] Historian Clara Snapp reports that this former schoolhouse was owned at the time by Judge James D. Shipman, whose first wife was Mary E. McCubbin.[490] Lewis C. McCubbin died on June 16, 1933 in Linn Creek and was buried at Freedom Cemetery, about three miles south of Passover.[491]

Ray McCubbin and his son Merrill ("Mac"), who lived in their house on the McCubbin farm, also moved to "new" Linn Creek. Merrill was ten years old at the time. After moving to Linn Creek, Ray worked as a carpenter and lived in a boarding house. After Lewis McCubbin's death in Linn Creek on June 16, 1933, Jemimah lived with her son Ray in Lebanon, Missouri, until Ray died on October 23, 1943, and was buried at Freedom Cemetery.[492] Jemimah then lived with her son, J. O. (Ollie) McCubbin, in Eldon, Missouri. She died on March 28, 1944 (or 1945, according to the gravestone), and was buried with her husband Lewis at Freedom Cemetery.[493]

James Merrill McCubbin

James Merrill ("Mac") McCubbin was born and raised by his parents, Ray and Leticia, in their house on the Lewis McCubbin farm near Passover. The 1920 U. S. census shows Merrill, at age two and a half years, living with his grandparents, Lewis and Jemimah, at their farm near Passover. A family photograph shows Merrill standing with Ray and Tish McCubbin and members of the Moulder family in Honey Run Creek or McCubbin's Ford, probably when Merrill was being baptized by his grandfather.[494] Merrill attended the old log school in Passover that his father and his aunts and uncles had also attended. A newspaper photo of the class of 1927-1928 at Passover School shows Merrill, aged eight years, kneeling in the front row. Of the thirty students in the photo, seven are DeGraffenreids and five are Salsmans.[495]

On September 20, 1941, James Merrill McCubbin married Leta Eileen Chalfant in Stoutland, Missouri. They had six children, born between 1942 and 1957. During World War II, Merrill served in the U. S. Coast Guard.[496] After the war he lived in Maine for many years, and while there wrote a small booklet, called *Wild Food & Other Outdoor Drivel*, about edible plants, fish, and animals. In this book, discussing the merits of yellow perch, he says "I have taken hundreds here in Maine up to 14 inches and one or two 16 inchers." He describes how to clean and cook perch, and he also tells how to make woodchuck stew and snapping-turtle stew, Maryland style.[497]

In January 1975, after a visit to the old home place, Merrill "Mac" McCubbin wrote: "Granddad [Lewis] McCubbin built the old log house in the background [of the 1930 photo] in 1869. The big catalpa tree was planted then by Grandma. The old log and stump is there yet as I found them while I was there last fall. There is a 12-inch sprout growing out of the stump. The old well curb and milk box is still there also the old hearthstone from the cabin. The cement footing I helped Grandpa put up the pole for the martin house is still there. Also, the old stone fence that was across the front yard. And over at the old house place where we lived [with his father and mother, Ray and Tish] I found the cellar Ma shut me in because I wouldn't go the first year of school I should have. Ma's folks also lived down there. Grandpa and Uncle Jim McCulley ran a blacksmith shop there. You can remember that I bet."[498]

Merrill McCubbin died on April 6, 1988, and is buried a few miles south of Passover at Freedom Cemetery, where his father Ray, his grandparents Lewis and Jemimah, and other former friends are also buried.[499]

Oklahoma

Before Oklahoma became a state, it was the home of sixty-seven Indian tribes, on reservations administered by the U. S. Department of Indian Affairs. After the Civil War, during which some of the tribes supported the Confederacy, the U. S. Congress federalized some of the reservation lands and prepared to open them to settlement by homesteaders. The lands in the central part of Oklahoma, which were never "assigned" as Indian reservations and were called Oklahoma Territory (as opposed to Indian Territory), were the first to open to settlement by a "land run" in 1889. The towns of Oklahoma City, Guthrie, Stillwater, and Perkins were among the new towns established at that time.[500] The Sac and Fox Indian Reservation and the Iowa Indian Reservation, south of the Cimarron River opposite the town of Perkins, were officially opened to settlement in 1891. The Cherokee Outlet (or Cherokee Strip), part of the Cherokee Reservation, was opened by a land run in September, 1893. The towns of Tryon and Glencoe were established after these land openings.[501] (The lands of the large Cherokee and Osage reservations were allocated to individual tribal members after 1907, under the federal Dawes Act, but were not opened to other settlers.)

Fred and Julie McCommon Wilson, whose daughter Bernice was married to C. B. (Bruell) McCubbin, moved from Camden County, Missouri, to the Perkins, Oklahoma area in March 1908. There, the Wilsons worked for a Mr. Golden and lived in the "little house, then yellow" that still sits back in the field just southwest of the present Jerry and Mary Coe farm on Highway 33 near Perkins. Then, in 1919, Fred Wilson and Mr. Golden went back to Camden County and helped Bruell and Bernice McCubbin and their three children move to Oklahoma.[502]

This two-story farmhouse, located one mile east and one mile north of the town of Tryon, Lincoln County, Oklahoma, is now abandoned but was the home of the Bruell McCubbin family after they arrived in 1908, according to the recollections of Pauline McCubbin. (Photo by the author.)

This family photo shows Bruell, Bernice, and Edman Gale McCubbin with their toddler, Glenn McCubbin, in about 1923, probably in the town of Tryon. (Collection of the author.)

At the time of this move, Bruell was 36 years old and Bernice was 28. Gale McCubbin was about 10, Pauline was 6, and Thelma was three.

The Wilsons may have helped Bruell McCubbin and his family find land after they arrived in the Perkins, Oklahoma area. The McCubbins settled on a farm located one mile north and one mile east of Tryon in Lincoln County. The farm had a house and outbuildings when they arrived, and Pauline had childhood memories of her father putting a new roof on the barn.[503] Both the two-story farmhouse and the barn are now abandoned but are still standing. This farm land, in the northwest quarter, section 12, township 16 north, range 3 east (160 acres) had been claimed as a federal homestead on December 30, 1901, by John N. Shoemaker.[504] This farm, like most of the other farms in the area, may have produced cotton. The McCubbins probably were leasing the land and operating the farm there. At some point, while living on this farm, Bruell took a job working at the Bellis Cotton Company cotton gin in the nearby town of Tryon.[505] A family photo shows Bernice, Bruell, Gale, and a very young Glenn McCubbin, probably in Tryon.

The land in the area, probably including the McCubbin farm, was formerly part of the Iowa Indian Reservation. After the Iowa Reservation was closed, some of the Iowa Indians acquired former reservation land and continued living in the area. Today, tribal members of the Iowa Tribe of Oklahoma have their own tribal government and cultural center in the town of Perkins. One of the stories that Bernice McCubbin later told her family after they moved to Glencoe was that, while living on the farm near Tryon, she was sometimes frightened by the sound of the Indians at their powwows "on the creek nearby."[506] The creek was probably Sand Creek, about one-half mile west of the McCubbin house.

Pauline and Gale McCubbin attended the rural Harmony school, which was located about 100 yards west of their house. Pauline remembered that her teacher, Miss Emma Hall, who was the first teacher at Harmony, roomed in the McCubbin home nearby.[507] "Harmony was a one room, one-teacher school. All eight grades were taught. In the early years the attendance would be in the middle thirties to the upper forties. Facilities were very primitive . . . a coal stove near the center of the classroom, water was carried in from the well in a bucket, no lights and outside restrooms."[508] A sign installed in 1924, on the front of the school building, read: "Harmony School, 1902, District No.16," with the motto "Excelsior." A photo published in the book *History of Lincoln County [Oklahoma]* shows the school, with the sign on the front, and thirty or so students gathered in front of the school, including Gale and Pauline McCubbin, named in the photo caption.[509]

Harmony School — The name of some of the children are: Floyd Hemphill standing on the left porch rail, Bert Scott standing on the right porch rail, Clespie Nickelson, Roy, Preston and Irene Matthews, Velma, Zola and Lola Hemphill, Alfred and Louie Tate, Evelyn, Mary and Harold, Tarlton, Theona and Florence Mote, Rhea Nickelson and her two small brothers, Mary Scott, Gale and Pauline McCubbin, Bernice Hagler and her two sisters, Leland and Lena Underwood, Zelma and Bertha Flannery, plus several that names cannot be recalled.

The Harmony School, shown here, was a one-room school where "all eight grades were taught." The caption in this 1924 photo lists the names of 24 of the children, including those of Gale and Pauline McCubbin. (From Lincoln County Historical Society, *History of Lincoln County*, p. 252.)

In about 1925, Bruell McCubbin and his family moved about thirty miles north from their farm in the Tryon area to the town of Glencoe, in Payne County, where Bruell worked as a cotton buyer and manager of the Bellis Company cotton gin.[510] As mentioned earlier, Glencoe had been established as a small farming community at the time of the Land Run which opened the Cherokee Strip to settlement in 1893. Town lots were first offered for sale in 1901, shortly after the railroad was completed into Glencoe.[511] It was at this time that the cotton gin was built near the railroad station. By the time of the 1930 U. S. census, Glencoe's population was 297. According to Glenn McCubbin, the family's first home in Glencoe was the stone house that is still standing on the east side of town near the highway 108.[512]

The M & K (McCubbin & Kincaid) Market, Glencoe, was owned and operated by Bruell (C. B.) McCubbin from about 1927 until his death in 1949. This family photo, made in about 1928, shows Bruell in the white shirt, center, and Edman Gale McCubbin on the far left. (From the collection of the author.)

Bruell McCubbin left his job at the cotton gin in about 1927, reportedly because of his allergy problems, and bought a grocery store, called the M & K (McCubbin and Kincaid) Market.[513] The grocery was on the south side of Main Street, just a couple of doors west of the Jake Bunn Mercantile store and across the street from the drug store. The grocery operated successfully, even during the depression years and World War II, serving the townspeople and the farming families in the surrounding area. Bruell and his family also kept chickens and had a small patch of corn at their home on the northwest side of town. Bruell also kept bees and harvested the honey for sale in the store.[514]

Doyle Wayne McCubbin, the youngest child, was born on September 30, 1931, after the family moved to Glencoe.[515] The children Pauline,

Gale, Glenn, Thelma, and Doyle all went to school there, and photos of their high school graduating classes are displayed at the Glencoe High School. Gale McCubbin worked for his father at the grocery store until 1936, when he and his wife Eva Marie Duncan and their son Donald Gene McCubbin moved to Stillwater, where Robert Gale McCubbin was born.[516]

Bruell McCubbin died on November 3, 1949, in Glencoe.[517] His widow Bernice worked as a hostess at one of the student residence halls at Oklahoma State University in Stillwater for 14 years before returning to Glencoe, where she died on January 10, 1965.[518] Funeral services were held at the First Baptist Church in Glencoe. Bernice McCubbin is buried beside her husband Bruell at the Glencoe Cemetery, south of Glencoe.[519]

Bruell was the last McCubbin in his line of descent from the founder, John Maccubbin of Anne Arundel County, Maryland, to move westward and continue the family tradition of being a farmer. When Bruell moved again to take a job in a cotton mill and then to become owner of a grocery store in Glencoe, he continued the tradition of taking a job in a new growing community to support his family.

Conclusions

The McCubbin/Maccubbin family, like many other American families, came to the colonies in America in search of greater economic and religious freedom and moved progressively westward as American homesteaders as new land opened on the western frontier. Throughout their history, the McCubbin families described here were farmers, had large families, and were active in their churches. Commonly, it was some of the younger members of the family who led the moves to find new land to support their families and establish their independence. As American homesteaders the McCubbins usually traveled with and settled with closely associated families, who helped them establish new communities in Maryland, Virginia, North Carolina, Kentucky, Illinois, Missouri, Oklahoma, California, and beyond. Descendants of the McCubbins and associated families still live in all of these places today.

Notes

1. https://www.familytreemakerdna.com. Y-DNA studies reported on the FTDN website show that the ancient ancestors of the McCubbins were the Celtic people who arrived in the British Isles from central Europe after about 2250 BC.
2. Alistair Moffatt, The Scots, a Genetic Journey. (Birlinn, Edinburgh, 2017), p.110, 119. The P-Celtic or Welch language survives in Cornwall, Wales, northwest Scotland, and Ireland, although it is now spoken by only a tiny remnant of the population. The Gaels who arrived in southwest. Scotland in about 900 AD spoke Q-Celtic or Gaelic.
3. Alistair Moffatt, The Scots, a Genetic Journey. 2017, p. 167-168. In the 700s, the Anglo-Saxons of Northumbria, in the present English-Scottish border area, expanded into present-day Dumfries and Galloway and established the Priory at Whithorn on the south coast.
4. Alistair Moffatt, The Scots, a Genetic Journey, 2017, p.196-197. The Gaelic leaders. perhaps because of their Viking heritage, became the princes and kings of Galloway.
5. George F. Black, The Surnames of Scottland, (New York Public Library, Birlinn,1946), p.482. The name "MacCubbin," is evidently of Gaelic origin because of the prefix "Mac" ("son of", in Gaelic). Black suggests that "Cubbin" was a corruption of "Gibbon".
6. Davidian Revolution, https://www.wikipedia.com, King David I, king of Scotland (1124-1153), introduced Norman-style feudalism and Anglo-Norman burghs and sheriffdoms into southwest Scotland, including Carrick.
7. #890-DNA-2 John "The Colonist" McCubbin, https://www.mccubbinhistory,com. Y-DNA data compiled and analyzed on the McCubbin family history website show that the American descendants of John Maccubbin of Maryland (DNA Group 2) have an identical or near-identical match with a McCubbin whose ancestors are buried near Tradunnock and who was told by family members that he is related to the McCubbins of Knockdolian.
8. William Robertson, Ayrshire: Its History and Historical Families, vol. 1, (Stephen & Pollack, Ayr, 1908), p. 21. Reprinted by Forgotten Books.com, London.
9. William Abercrummie, A Description of Carrict, the Geographical Collections Relating to Scotland Collected by Walter MacFarlane of the Ilk, Esquire, and Reprinted Subsequently as Carrick in 1696, with comments by Dave Killicoat, December 2002, https://www.maybole.org/history/books/abercrummie/carrick1696. Rev. Abercrummie, the retired minister of the church in Maybole, wrote in 1696 about Carrick and its land-owning families from his personal

knowledge and with definite opinions. He apparently admired the gentry, including the McCubbins of Knockdolian, and described their properties in some detail.

10. Abercrummie, A Description of Carrict. Also, James Paterson, History of the Counties of Ayr & Wigton [Scotland], Volume II: Carrick, James Stille, Edinburgh 1864. Paterson, who wrote many years after Abercrummie, describes Carrick's history and families based on land records, wills, and church records.
11. Smyson, 1660, cited in Black, The Surnames of Scotland, 1946, p. 393. This rhyme, which Illustrates the power of the Kennedy clan in 1660, has been quoted by historians many times. The word "cruives" in the rhyme means "livestock pen" in Old Scots.
12. David Drynan and T. Kennedy Drynan, History of Knockdolian, VII. Scottish Notes and Queries, vol. 53, no. 4 (December, 1928), p. 53. Also, Charters of the Abbey of Crossraguel, v. 1, 38, 39, https://www.mccubbinhistory.info, Miscellany. As a tenant, John Makcubyn occupied the property and must have paid rent to his feudal superior.
13. Drynan and Drynan, History of Knockdolian, v. VI, p. 53. Also, Dougal at Tradunnock, Charters of the Abbey of Crossraguel, May 20, 1492, v. V1, 38,39, August 24, 1404, http://www.mccubbinhistory.info, Miscellany. The owner of a property is recorded as "of" that property, whereas the person who lived in the property but did not own it is designated as "in" the property.
14. Drynan and Drynan, History of Knockdolian, v. VI, p. 53. Thomas McCubbin becomes full owner by sasine. A shilling was about one twentieth of a pound sterling.
15. 1619 John McCubbine & Archibald McCubbine, Secretary's Register RS 12/1 f.290 recorded 22 January 1619 (in Latin), https://www.mccubbinhistory.info, Miscellany. John, the eldest son of Archibald, is recognized as heir to Tradunnock by sasine.
16. John by sasine. Edinburg Commissary Court Register of Tenements (cc 8/8110), recorded 20/2/1583, https://www.mccubbinfamily.info, Miscellany.
17. 1606 John McCubeine, Secretary"s Register for Ayrshire and Bailliaries of Kyle, Carrick, and Cunningham, RS11/1 f. 359, recorded 4 September 1606 (in Latin), https://www.mccubbinhistory.info, Miscellany. A contract of marriage between John MacCubeine of Tradunnock and Jonet Kennedy, daughter of Alexander Kennedy of Drummelane dated 2 January 1606. Paterson, 1864, p. 209, reports that castle of the Drummelane was located near the Girvan River on the present estate of the Kilkerran Family.
18. Paterson, History of the Counties of Ayr and Wigton, p. 209. The Kennedys of Drummelane claimed descent from John Kennedy, "second of the three elder sons of Sir Gilbert Kennedy of Dunure", as were the Kennedys of Cove, and were a sub-branch of the Kennedys of Culzean.
19. Paterson, History of the Counties of Ayr and Wigton, p. 214-215. Jonet Kennedy is mentioned as "John McCubbin"s wf" in the will of Jonet's father, Alexander Kennedy.
20. 1620 Johnne McCubine in Killnq[uhai]r in the Parish of Kirkoswald," Glasgow Commissary Court, cc 9/7/17, recorded 11 July 1621 & 6 August 1622, https://www.mccubbinhistory.info>, Miscellany. Also, Wills, Glasgow Commissary Court Register of Testaments, cc 9/7/17, recorded 4 November 1620, https://

www.mccubbinhistory.info, Wills. John died in 1620. John's will showed that he was a wealthy man, with debts of farm products and money owed to him. A merk was worth 2/3rds of a Scots pound and after 1600 a Scots pound was worth 1/12 of a pound Sterling.

21. "1631 Fergus McCubine," Secretaries Register, RS12/5 f.2 recorded 1 January 1631 (in Latin), https://www.mccubbinhistory.info, Miscellany. Fergus was recognized as the heir to Tradunnock in a precept by John Hamilton of Bargany, RS12/5 f.2, recorded January 1, 1631

22. Fergus married Margaret Kennedy, RS12/4 f.668, recorded December 24, 1630, https://www.mccubbinhistory.info, Miscellany.

23. Paterson, History of the Counties of Ayr & Wigton, p. 272-273, 277-278. Paterson describes the House of Kirkmichael as "a pretty commodious house, within a short space of the church of the same." The Kirkmichaels claimed to be descended from David Kennedy, who was son of John Kennedy of Dunure and the first Earl of Cassillis.

24. John Maccubbin of Maryland, #80-DNA-2, https://www.mccubbinhistory.info. That John Maccubbin was the son of Fergus and Margaret is based on DNA evidence showing that American descendants of John have an "exact or near exact match" with Alan Robert McCubbin, whose family headstone is in Dailly, near Tradunnock, and who was told by his great-grand uncle that he was related to the McCubbins. John's calculated time of birth is near the time when Fergus and Margaret were married at Traddunnock. Drynan and Drynan, McCubbins of Tradunnock, v. VI, p. 53.

26. https://www.mccubbinhistory.info, John "the Colonist" McCubbin.

27. Doug Goldie, pers. comm., November 20 and 23, 2018.

28. Doug Goldie, pers. comm., November 20 and 23, 2018. Doug Goldie, a descendant of the Goddies (Goldies) of Tradunnock, provided this author a chronological summary of the records from the late 1600s to the 1800s.

29. William Robertson, Ayrshire: Its History and Historic Families, vol. 1, p. 151-153. Because of their role in the reprisal against the Campbells, the Kennedys of Bargany, Drummelane, and Kirkmichael were charged with murder. At about the same time, in 1528, "Fergus Makcubyn and John Makecubyn his son" also were arraigned for murder, probably because they were involved in the feud in support of their friends, the Drummelanes and the Kirkmichaels (Black, 1946, p. 482). It is not known how these Makcubyns were related to the McCubbins of Tradunnock.

30. Black, The Surnames of Scotland, p. 482.

31. Paterson, History of the Counties of Ayr & Wigton, v. II, p. 36-31, 193-194, 335. Robertson, Ayrshire: Its History and Historic Families, p. 22. The rescue of the Commendator by Bargany may have been motived in part by the fact that the Commendator, Allan Stewart, was the brother of Bargany's wife.

32. Paterson, History of the Counties of Ayr & Wigton, v. II, p. 56-60, 195-196.

33. Paterson, History of the Counties of Ayr & Wigton, v. II, p. 63-64, 196-197.

34. Robertson, Ayrshire: Its History and Historic Families, v. 1, p. 185-187. In 1611 a jury found the laird of Auchindrane and his son to be guilty of the murder of Thomas Kennedy of Culzean and both were executed. Bargany's brother, who also was implicated in the murder, had fled the country.

35. Paterson, History of the Counties of Ayr & Wigton, v. II, p. 69-70, 196-199.

36. Robertson, Ayrshire: Its History and Historic Counties, p. 242-243.
37. Imbrie, John D., no date, p. 107-118, https://www.aanhsorg.files.wordpress.com. The Carrick Covenant of 1628 was signed by 87 men, including the McAlexanders, Cathcarts, Fergussons, the Kennedys of Drummelane, and the Kennedys of Kirkmichael.
38. Drynan and Drynan, History of Knockdolian, v. VI, p. 53. Robertson, Ayrshire: Its History and Historic Families, p. 250.
39. Robertson, Ayrshire: Its History and Historic Families, p. 249.
40. David Dobson, Scots on the Chesapeake, 1621-1776, Revised edition, (Genealogical Publishing Company, Baltimore Maryland, 2012).
41. 1653 Fergus McCubbin, Acquisition of Knockdolian, Papers of the Cathcart Family of Genoch and Knockdolian, GD180/44 Discharge (receipt) https://www.mccubbinhistory.info, Miscellany. Records the purchase of the 20-pound lands of Knockdolian and the 10-merk lands of Glentig by Fergus MCubbin in Balhamie from John Kennedy of Kirkmichael in May 1653 for 32,000 merks. A merk was worth 2/3rds of a Scots pound, which in turn was worth 1/12th of a pound Sterling.
42. Drynan and Drynan, History of Knockdolian, v. VI, p. 70.
43. Nigel Tranter, The Fortified House in Scotland, vol. 5, North and West Scotland and Miscellaneous, (W & R Chambers Ltd. Edinburgh and London, 1970), p. 216-217. Mike Salter, The Castles of South-west Scotland, (Folly Publications, Malvern Worc., 2006), p. 50-51.
44. Abercrummie, A Description of Carrict, p. 8.
45. Drynan and Drynan, History of Knockdolian, v. VI, 3rd series, VIII, p. 70. The coat of arms of Fergus McCubbin is located on the outside, above the door, and that of Margaret Kennedy is on the inside, on the back wall, as observed by Donald McCubbin. A drawing of McCubbin coat of arms, with the hawk and the motto "Prey to None", is reproduced in the section, "McCubbins of Knockdolian," McCubbin family history website https://www.mccubbinhistory.info.
46. Robertson, Ayrshire: Its History and Historic Families, v. 1, p. 269.
47. "Fergus, the Mystery Man?," https://www.mccubbinhistory.info. Drynan and Drynan, History of Knockdolian, IX, vol. VI, 3rd series, May, p. 90-91
48. Drynan and Drynan, History of Knockdolian, VIII, vol I, 3rd series, p. 71.
49. Robertson, Ayrshire: Its History and Historic Families, p. 274-280.
50. Dobson, Scots on the Chesapeake, 1621-1776. Introduction.
51. Paterson, History of the Counties of Ayr & Wigton, v. II, p. 164.
52. William McConel obituary, October 23, 1902, clipping from unknown newspaper; received from Douglas Calderwood, Knockdolian Estate, pers. comm. to Donald McCubbin.
53. https://www.thepeerage.com, person page 10377; also enwikipedia.org/wiki/ArthurValerianWellesley, "8th Duke of Wellington".
54. Norman K. Risjord, Builders of Annapolis: Enterprise and Politics in a Colonial Capital. (Maryland Historical Society, Baltimore.1997), p. xiii.
55. Caleb Dorsey, "Original Land Grants of the South Side of Severn River," Maryland Historical Magazine, vol. 53, no. 4 (December,1958), p. 394.
56. Anthony D. Lindauer, From Paths to Plats: the Development of Annapolis, 1651-1718, (The Maryland State Archives and the Maryland Historical Trust, 1997), p. 2
57. Lindauer, From Paths to Plats: the Development of Annapolis, 1651-1718, 1997, p. 3.

58. Dorsey, "Original Land Grants of the South Side of Severn River," p. 397-400
59. Rudolf Loeser, "John Maccubbin of Anne Arundel County and His Children," Maryland Genealogical Society Bulletin, vol. 40, no. 2 (Spring 1999), p. 197.
60. J. D. Warfield, The Founders of Anne Arundel and Howard Counties, Maryland: A Genealogical and Biographical Review from Wills, Deeds, and Church Records, (Kohn and Pollack, Publishers, Baltimore MD), 1905, p. 33.
61. Elizabeth B. Anderson, Annapolis: A Walk through History, (Tidewater Publishers, Centreville MD, 1984), p. 15.
62. Lindauer, From Paths to Plats, p. 9.
63. Anderson, Annapolis, p. 15.
64. Anderson, Annapolis, p. 16.
65. Risjord, Builders of Annapolis, p. 24-26.
66. Anderson, Annapolis, p. 18.
67. Anderson, Annapolis, p. 19.
68. "Danced with Washington, Mrs. James McCubbin of Annapolis Enjoyed This Honor," New York Times, May 19, 1895, http://query.nytimes.com/mem/archivefree/pdf?res=F70E16FA3C5811. Also, P. H. Magruder, "A Walk through Annapolis in Bygone Days," U. S. Naval Institute Proceedings, Annapolis MD, 1931, which contains a print showing Mrs. Maccubbin on the arm of General Washington, p. xvii.
69. Anderson, Annapolis.
70. George Norbury Mackenzie, ed., Colonial Families of the United States of America, vol. IV. (Genealogical Publishing Co., Baltimore MD, 1966), p. 349.
71. Anderson, Annapolis, p. 36
72. Anderson, Annapolis, p. 117, 119-121.
73. Donna M. Ware, Anne Arundel's Legacy: The Historic Properties of Anne Arundel County. (Environmental and Special Project Division, Office of Planning and Zoning, Anne Arundel County, Annapolis MD, 1990).
74. Donald McCubbin, personal observations on a visit to the Brampton house in June, 2002.
75. Dorsey, "Original Land Grants of the South Side of Severn River," p. 394.
76. Dorsey, "Original Land Grants of the South Side of Severn River," map and p. 397-400.
77. Loeser, "John Maccubbin of Anne Arundel County and His Children," p. 159. Patent record, 'Ellis Browne', v. 11, p. 135-136, Maryland State Archives, Annapolis, Maryland.
78. Loeser, "John Maccubbin of Anne Arundel County and His Children," p. 159, 196.
79. Ware, "Anne Arundel's Legacy: The Historic Properties of Anne Arundel County," p. 37.
80. Loeser, "John Maccubbin of Anne Arundel County and His Children," p. 159.
81. Risjord, Builders of Annapolis, p. xiii-iv.
82. Carville V. Earle, The Evolution of a Tidewater Settlement System, All Hallows Parish, Maryland, 1650-1783, (The University of Chicago Department of Geography Research Paper No. 170, Chicago ILL, 1975), p. 27. Also cited in Loeser, p. 160.
83. Risjord, Builders of Annapolis, p. xiv
84. Risjord, Builders of Annapolis, p. 59-60.

85. Loeser, John Maccubbin of Anne Arundel County and His Children, p. 159.
86. Loeser, John Maccubbin of Anne Arundel County and His Children, p. 159.
87. Loeser, John Maccubbin of Anne Arundel County and His Children, p. 161.
88. Loeser, John Maccubbin of Anne Arundel County and His Children, p. 162.
89. Ware, 1990, p. 9-11.
90. Loeser, John Maccubbin of Anne Arundel County and His Children, p. 161-162.
91. Loeser, John Maccubbin of Anne Arundel County and His Children, p. 162.
92. Loeser, Anne Arundel's Legacy, p. 198.
93. Dorsey, Original Land Grants of the South Side of Severn River, p. 397-400.
94. Lindauer, From Paths to Plats, p. 10.
95. Dorsey, Original Land Grants of the South Side of Severn River, p. 397-400.
96. Loeser, John Maccubbin of Anne Arundel County and His Children, p. 165.
97. Jane W. McWilliams, Howard's Inheritance (AA0136), (Historical Research and Documentation, Annapolis MD, May 1996), p. 1.
98. Warfield, The Founders of Anne Arundel and Howard Counties, Maryland, p. 31.
99. Reaney Kelly, Quakers in the Founding of Anne Arundel County, Maryland, (Maryland Historical Society. Baltimore MD, 1963).
100. Kim Keck, Friends, Tobacco, and Slavery: First Patuxent Meeting,1666-1817, manuscript dated 2003, p. 7, Patuxent Friends Meeting website, https://www.patuxentfriends.org.
101. Kelly, Quakers in the Founding of Anne Arundel County, Maryland, p. 337.
102. Warfield, The Founders of Anne Arundel and Howard Counties, Maryland, p. 31.
103. Jacobsen, 1966.
104. Loeser, John Maccubbin of Anne Arundel County and His Children, p. 192-193.
105. Warfield, The Founders of Anne Arundel and Howard Counties, Maryland, p. 31.
106. Lois Green Carr and Russell R. Menard, Immigration and Opportunity: The Freedman in Early Colonial Maryland in the Chesapeake in the Seventeen Century, Thad W. Tate and David L. Ammerman, eds, 1979, p. 207; quoted by Loeser, 1999, p. 163.
107. Kelly, Quakers in the Founding of Anne Arundel County, Maryland, p. 344.
108. Kelly, Quakers in the Founding of Anne Arundel County, Maryland,1963, p. 344.
109. Loeser, John McCubbin of Anne Arundel County and His Children, p. 162, 169. Loeser reports the information he used to estimate dates of birth, marriage, and death where birth records are lacking. Earlier estimates by other authors and family genealogists, such as Hugh Jenkins, are generally close to those by Loeser.
110. Luther W. Welsh, Ancestral Colonial Families: Genealogy of the Welsh and Hyatt Families of Maryland and their Kin, (Lambert Moon Printing Co., Independence MO), 1928, p. 169; Warfield, The Founders of Anne Arundel and Howard Counties, Maryland, 1905, p. 177.
111. Dorsey, Original Land Grants of the South Side of Severn River, 1958, p. 398-400.
112. Jane W. McWilliams, Howard's Inheritance (AA0136), Historical Research and Documentation, Annapolis MD, May 1996, p. 1. Also, Kelly, 1963, p. 89-81.
113. Loeser, John Maccubbin of Anne Arundel County and His Children, p. 170-171.
114. Loeser, John Maccubbin of Anne Arundel County and His Children, p. 171.

115. Welsh, Ancestral Colonial Families, p. 169.
116. Harry Wright Newman, Anne Arundel Gentry, Vol. 2, (published by the author, Annapolis MD), p. 231
117. Hugh Jenkins genealogy, personal communication. Jenkins compiled a thorough, mostly documented genealogy or family tree. This tree, exported to Donald McCubbin as a Family Treemaker file and. with added information by Donald McCubbin for more recent generations, has been upload to https://www.ancestry.com.
118. Loeser, John Maccubbin of Anne Arundel County and His Children, p. 162.
119. Welsh, Ancestral Colonial Families, p. 169.
120. Loeser, John Maccubbin of Anne Arundel County and His Children, p. 169, 201.
121. Risjord, Builders of Annapolis, p. 77-78.
122. Michael F. Trostel, Mount Clare: Being an Account of the Seat Built by Charles Carroll, Barrister, upon His Lands at Patapsco, (National Society of the Colonial Dames of America in the State of Maryland), 1981 (date of acknowledgements), diagram inside back cover. The ancestry of Eleanor is not discussed in the text of the book, and the source of the information on the diagram is not identified.
123. Loeser, John Maccubbin of Anne Arundel County and His Children, p. 162-163.
124. Loeser, John Maccubbin of Anne Arundel County and His Children, p. 162-163.
125. Loeser, John Maccubbin of Anne Arundel County and His Children, p. 162.
126. Loeser, John Maccubbin of Anne Arundel County and His Children, p. 163-165.
127. Helen W. Ridgely, Historic Graves of Maryland and the District of Columbia, (Genealogical Publishing Co., Baltimore), 1967, p. 9. Originally published by the Grafton Press, New York, 1908.
128. Ridgely, Historic Graves of Maryland and the District of Columbia, p. 9.
129. Nomination Form for the National Register of Historic Places, "The Old Maccubbin House at Brampton," no date.
130. Land-title abstract for Brampton, copied from the files of the Anne Arundel County Planning Office for Donald McCubbin.
131. Welsh, Ancestral Colonial Families, p. 145.
132. Welsh, Ancestral Colonial Families, p. 148-149. Loeser, John Maccubbin of Anne Arundel County and His Children, p. 166.
133. Loeser, John Maccubbin of Anne Arundel County and His Children, p. 167.
134. Loeser, John Maccubbin of Anne Arundel County and His Children, p. 167.
135. Loeser, John Maccubbin of Anne Arundel County and His Children, p. 167.
136. Loeser, John Maccubbin of Anne Arundel County and His Children, p. 167.
137. Loeser, John Maccubbin of Anne Arundel County and His Children, p. 187.
138. Loeser, John Maccubbin of Anne Arundel County and His Children, p. 167-168.
139. Loeser, John Maccubbin of Anne Arundel County and His Children, p. 168, 201.
140. Loeser, John Maccubbin of Anne Arundel County and His Children, p. 170-172.
141. Loeser, John Maccubbin of Anne Arundel County and His Children, p. 171-172. Also, F. Edward Wright, Anne Arundel County Church Records of the 17th and 18th Centuries, (Family Line Publications, Westminster, Maryland), no date, p. 71.
142. Loeser, John Maccubbin of Anne Arundel County and His Children, p. 172.
143. Robert E. McCubbin, pers. comm., April 2001, letter to Donald McCubbin.
144. Loeser, John Maccubbin of Anne Arundel County and His Children, p. 169-170.
145. Loeser, John Maccubbin of Anne Arundel County and His Children, p. 169.
146. Nomination Form for the National Register of Historic Places, "The Old

McCubbin House at Brampton," no date.
147. Ware, Anne Arundel's Legacy, p. 51-52.
148. Loeser, John Maccubbin of Anne Arundel County and His Children, p. 169.
149. Loeser, John Maccubbin of Anne Arundel County and His Children, p. 172-173.
150. Loeser, John Maccubbin of Anne Arundel County and His Children, p. 172.
151. Risjord, Builders of Annapolis, p. 23.
152. Risjord, Builders of Annapolis, p. 24; Gary 1953, p. 313. City lots were laid out and numbers assigned to them by 1695 according to Lindauer, 1997.
153. Joy Gary, "Patrick Creagh of Annapolis," Maryland Historical Magazine, vol. 48, no. 4, December 1953, p. 314-316.
154. Trostel, Mount Clare, p. 17-18.
155. Gary, "Patrick Creagh of Annapolis," p. 320. The Annapolis harbor was then much larger than that which serves the present City Dock. Part of it has since been filled in and now is part of a parking lot.
156. Gary, "Patrick Creagh of Annapolis," p. 321
157. Gary, "Patrick Creagh of Annapolis," p. 322-323. Risjord, Builders of Annapolis, p. 35-36.
158. MacKenzie, Colonial Families of the United States of America, vol. IV, p. 351
159. MacKenzie, Colonial Families of the United States pf America, vol. IV, p. 351.
160. Gary, Patrick Creagh of Annapolis, p. 323.
161. Gary, Patrick Creagh of Annapolis, p. 323; Anderson, Annapolis, p. 56.
162. Gary, Patrick Creagh of Annapolis, p. 325; Risjord, Builders of Annapolis, p. 36.
163. Gary, Patrick Creagh of Annapolis, p. 321.
164. Gary, Patrick Creagh of Annapolis, p. 323.
165. Gary, Patrick Creagh of Annapolis, p. 320.
166. Anderson, Annapolis, p. 117. When Donald McCubbin visited there in June, 2001, the house was a bed-and-breakfast. We were given a tour of part of the house.
167. Gary, Patrick Creagh of Annapolis, p. 324.
168. Loeser, John Maccubbin of Anne Arundel County and His Family, p. 205.
169. Gary, Patrick Creagh of Annapolis, p. 325.
170. Gary, Patrick Creagh of Annapolis, p. 325.
171. Loeser, John Maccubbin of Anne Arundel County and His Family, p. 205.
172. Loeser, John Maccubbin of Anne Arundel County and His Family, p. 172
173. Gary, Patrick Creagh of Annapolis, p. 324-325; Risjord, Builders of Annapolis, p. 36.
174. "Abstract of title for Brampton," files of Anne Arundel County Planning Office, copy in personal files of Donald McCubbin.
175. Anderson, Annapolis. p. 117; also, pers. observation by Donald McCubbin on visit in June 2002.
176. Gary, Patrick Creagh of Annapolis, p. 325.; Anderson, Annapolis, p. 119-121.
177. MacKenzie, Colonial Families of the United States, vol. IV, p. 351.
178. Robert Harry McIntire, Annapolis Maryland Families, (Gateway Press, Baltimore MD, 1979), p. 441.
179. Ridgely, Historic Graves of Maryland and the District of Columbia, p. 10.
180. Ridgely, Historic Graves of Maryland and the District of Columbia, p. 10.
181. New York Times, newspaper article, May 19, 1895.
182. MacKenzie, Colonial Families of the United States, vol. IV, p. 361.

183. Magruder, A Walk Through Annapolis in Bygone Days, p. 102. The author, Secretary of the U. S. Naval Academy, describes Martha Mackubin's attendance at the ball honoring Washington and also reports seeing the painting of Martha and General Washington at the ball and a portrait of Martha in the home of the Walton family, who were descendants of Martha. The painting of Martha Mackubin and Washington is reproduced on page xviii.
184. Loeser, John Maccubbin of Anne Arundel County and His Family, p. 184, 215.
185. Loeser, John Maccubbin of Anne Arundel County and His Family, p. 184.
186. Loeser, John Maccubbin of Anne Arundel County and His Family, p. 184.
187. Loeser, John Maccubbin of Anne Arundel County and His Family, p. 184.
188. MacKenzie, Colonial Families of the United States of America, vol. IV, p. 354.
189. Loeser, John Maccubbin of Anne Arundel County and His Family, p. 184-185; https://www.findagrave.com, All Hallows Churchyard, Birdsville, Anne Arundel.
190. Ware, Anne Arundel's Legacy, p. 51-52. The South River Club claims to be the first English-style social club in America and is still operating today. The club building and the separate kitchen building were listed on the National Register in 1972.
191. Loeser, John Maccubbin of Anne Arundel County and His Family, p. 185-185.
192. Robert Barnes, Maryland Marriages, 1634-1777, (Genealogical Publishing Co., Baltimore MD, 1975), p. 114; Welsh, Ancestral Colonial Families, p. 171.
193. Trostel, Mount Clare, p. 4-5. A portrait of Mary Clare Carroll is also displayed at Mount Clare House, now a museum.
194. Risjord, Builders of Annapolis, p. 61.
195. Risjord, Builders of Annapolis, p. 77.
196. Risjord, Builders of Annapolis, p. 59.
197. Trostel, Mount Clare, p. 4.
198. Warfield, The Founder of Anne Arundel and Howard Counties, p. 178.
199. Trostel, Mount Clare, p. 4-5.
200. Anderson, Annapolis, p. 36.
201. Trostel, Mount Clare, p. XVI.
202. Trostel, Mount Clare, p. 2.
203. Anderson, Annapolis, p. 36.
204. Donald McCubbin, personal observation on visit to Carroll House, Annapolis, in June 2001.
205. MacKenzie, Colonial Families of the United States of America, vol. IV, p. 349.
206. Trostel, Mount Clare, p. 17-18.
207. Inventory form, Maryland Historical Trust, "Java, Contee", undated. Describes ruins of the house at the former plantation, Squirrel Neck.
208. Donald McCubbin, pers. observation on visit to the former plantation, Squirrel Neck, in June 2001.
209. Loeser, John Maccubbin of Anne Arundel County and His Family, p. 215.
210. Anderson, Annapolis, p. 18-19.
211. Daughters of the American Revolution, Patriot Index,1990.
212. MacKenzie, Colonial Families of the United States, vol. IV, p. 350.
213. Trostel, Mount Clare, 91-92.
214. Hugh Jenkins, genealogical database, personal communication fo Donald McCubbin. A transcription of the will of Nicholas1 McCubbin is included in the notes for Nicholas1.

215. MacKenzie, Colonial Families of the United States, vol. IV, p. 355; Welsh, Ancestral Colonial Families, p. 172; and Mary Keysor Meyer, Divorces and Names Changed in Maryland, by Act of the Legislature, 1634-1854, p. 85.
216. Welsh, Ancestral Colonial Families, p. 172.
217. Warfield, The Founders of Anne Arundel and Howard Counties, Maryland, p. 177.
218. MacKenzie, Colonial Families of the United States, vol. IV, p. 355; Warfield, The Founders of Anne Arundel and Howard Counties, Maryland, p. 177; Welsh, Ancestral Colonial Families, p. 172.
219. Trostel, Mount Clare, p. 83.
220. Trostel, Mount Clare, p. 32.
221 Mount Clare House Museum, https://www.mountclare.org. Summary of the life of Nicholas Maccubbin Carroll (1751-1812).
222. Harry Wright Newman, Anne Arundel Gentry, a Genealogical History of Some Early Families of Anne Arundel County, Maryland, vol. 3, (self-published, Annapolis MD, 1979), p. 160.
223. Trostel, Mount Clare, p. 83.
224. Trostel, Mount Clare, p. 91.
225. Trostel, Mount Clare, p. 86-87.
226. Ware, Anne Arundel's Legacy, p. 37-39.
227. https://www.findagrave.com, All Hallows Episcopal Church, Birdsville, Ann Arundel County, MD. Memorials for Mary Ann (52759249) and Samuel MacCubbin (52759310) are maintained by Margaret.
228. Ware, Anne Arundel's Legacy, p. 25.
229. Loeser, John Maccubbin of Anne Arundel County and His Family, p. 187.
230. Loeser, John Maccubbin of Anne Arundel County and His Family, p. 188-189.
231. Loeser, John Maccubbin of Anne Arundel County and His Family, p. 188.
232. Loeser, John Maccubbin of Anne Arundel County and His Family, p. 188.
233. Loeser, John Maccubbin of Anne Arundel County and His Family, p. 188.
234. Anderson, Annapolis.1984.
235. Loeser, John Maccubbin of Anne Arundel County and His Family, p. 189-190.
236. Lindauer, From Paths to Plats, p. 14-15.
237. Loeser, John Maccubbin of Anne Arundel County and His Family, p. 180.
238. Loeser, John Maccubbin of Anne Arundel County and His Family, p. 180-181.
239. Hugh Jenkins genealogy database on Donald McCubbin's familytreemaker file.
240. Newman, Anne Arundel Gentry, v. 3, p. 153.
241. Loeser, John Maccubbin of Anne Arundel County and His Family, p. 183.
242. Loeser, John Maccubbin of Anne Arundel County and His Family, p. 180.
243. Loeser, John Maccubbin of Anne Arundel County and His Family, p. 181.
244. Loeser, John Maccubbin of Anne Arundel County and His Family, p. 181, 212.
245. Loeser, John Maccubbin of Anne Arundel County and His Family, p. 181.
246. Robert E. McCubbin, pers. comm., May 22, 2001, July 12, 2001.
247. Letters to the Baltimore Sun, May and November, 1906; in Loeser, 1999, p. 211.
248. Loeser, John Maccubbin of Anne Arundel County and His Family, p. 211.
249. Loeser, John Maccubbin of Anne Arundel County and His Family, p. 181; Newman, Anne Arundel Gentry, v. 3, p. 154.
250. Wright, Edward, Anne Arundel Church Records of the 17th and 18th Centuries, 1990.
251. Hugh Jenkins genealogy. Jenkins provides no documentation for this origin of

William2.
252. Robert E. McCubbin, pers. comm., April 15, 2001. Handwritten records state that William MacCubbin, wheelwright, of Ann Arundel County received from Enoch Conly his father-in-law Strawberry Plains in 1747,.and that in 1748 William MacCubin of Ann Arundel Co. sold to Enoch Conly of Lancaster County, PA, Strawberry Plains for five schillings. Records showing the time and place of marriage between William2 and Eleanor Conley were not found.
253. Patricia Anderson, Abstract of Frederick County, MD land records, bk. E, folio 908-910, record from Maryland State Archives, 1995, p. 80. Copy received from Robert E. McCubbin, May 22, 2001.
254. Maud Carter Clement, The History of Pittsylvania County, Virginia, (J. P. Hill Company, Lynchburg VA, 1929), p. 34-35.
255. Clement, The History of Pittsylvania County, Virginia, p. 37, p. 46-47.
256. Clement, The History of Pittsylvania County, Virginia, p. 46.
257. Clement, The History of Pittsylvania County, Virginia, p. 78-88.
258 Parke Rouse, Jr., The Great Wagon Road, (The Dietz Press, Richmond VA, reprinted 2008), p. 85-89.
259. Clement, The History of Pittsylvania County, Virginia, p. 74-75.
260. Clement, The History of Pittsylvania County, Virginia, p. 44.
261. Clement, The History of Pittsylvania County, Virginia, p. 125 and 126, footnote.
262. Pittsylvania County, Virginia, land records, Libre 8, Folio 278; in Hugh Jenkins genealogy, personal communication.
263. Pittsylvania County, Virginia, land records, Libre 8, Folio 278; in Patterson, 1988, p. 146.
264. Alta Kennard Patterson (ed. Virginia Fern Mithell), Kennard, King, Knight, Hardin, Goodin: Their Ancestors & Descendants, Genealogical report, self-published, and printed by (BookCrafters1988, Chelsea MI, 1988), p. 143-147.
265. Pittsylvania County, Virginia land records; deed book 8, p. 278, in Patterson, 1988, p. 146.
266. Clement, The History of Pittsylvania County, Virginia, p. 126, footnote.
267. Clement, The History of Pittsylvania County, Virginia, p. 44.
268. Clement, The History of Pittsylvania County, Virginia, p. 125-126.
269. Muster Rolls and Other Records of Service of Maryland Troops in the American Revolution, 1775-1783, Baltimore Maryland Historical Society, (Lord Baltimore Press, Baltimore, 1900), p. 52. Also, Craig Davidson, family genealogy reports, 1966.
270. Journal and Correspondence of the Maryland Council of Safety, August 29, 1775-July 6, 1776.
271. Jonesboro, Tennessee land records, bk. 8, p. 215.
272. Zachariah McCubbin tombstone, Old Irish Cemetery, Tazewell TN, https://www.findagrave.com, memorial 63645771.
273. Sarah Lane tombstone, Old Irish Cemetery, Tazewell TN, http://www.findagrave.com, memorial 151999323.
274. Pittsylvania County, Virginia, Public Service Claims, in Patterson, 1988, p. 146.
275. Early Families of the North Carolina Counties of Rockingham and Stokes, with Revolutionary Service, compiled by James Hunter Chapter, Daughters of the American Revolution. Madison North Carolina, 1977, p. 82. Nicholas's statement and supporting testimony for Mary's pension application are summarized in

this source. Documents are available in Revolutionary War Records, Nicholas McCubbin, N. C., series M805, roll 566, image 549, file W3574, page 1-15, Family Search Library.
276. Nicholas McCubbin/Nancy Jones marriage record, Pittsylvania County, VA.
277. DAR record 429341, Virginia State Archives; cited in Patterson, 1988, p. 277.
278. Early Families of the North Carolina Counties of Rockingham and Stokes, with Revolutionary Service, James Hunter Chapter DAR, 1977, p. 80-81. Claim 1836, National DAR 250045 and 429341, bounty land warrant 265-160-55, cited in Patterson, 1988, p. 162-164.
279. Gleason McCubbin, no date?, John P. Little (McCubbin), His Ancestors and His Descendants, p 43.
280. McCubbin household, 1790 U.S. Census, Anne Arundel County, Maryland; cited in Patterson, 1988, p. 143. John McCubbin and Sappho London may be listed in this census.
281. Robert W. Barnes, Baltimore County Families, 1659-1759, (Genealogical Publishing Co., Baltimore MD, 1989). Reprinted ty Clearfield,1996, p. 436-437.
282. Hugh Jenkins, genealogy database, personal communication to Donald McCubbin.
283. Gleason McCubbin, no date? p. 43.
284. Battle of Guilford Courthouse, http://www.wikipedia.com.
285. Robert W. Carter, Jr., "A History of Wolf Island Primitive Baptist Church," Journal of Rockingham County History and Genealogy, vol. IX, no. 1, June 1984, p. 3.
286. Carter, A History of Wolf Island Primitive Baptist Church, p. 3.
287. Carter, A History of Wolf Island Primitive Baptist Church, p. 2.
288. Rockingham County, Virginia, deed book, bk B, p. 15.
289. Rockingham County, Virginia, deed book, bk C, p. 216
290. Rockingham County, Virginia, deed book, bk D, p. 205
291. Rockingham County, Virginia, deed book, bk E, p. 298; in Patterson, 1988, p. 146.
292. Patterson, Kennard, King, Knight, Hardin, Goodin, p. 150-159. The birth dates of James and Polly and all 13 of their children were recorded in a family record which was copied from the family bible by son Nicholas McCubbin and preserved in the files of John C. McCubbin, Fresno CA.
293. Patterson, Kennard, King, Knight, Hardin, Goodin, p. 137.
294. Gleason Moss McCubbin, Nicholas Blind Nick McCubbin, 1780-1855: His Ancestors and His Descendants,1980, p. 43.
295. Rockingham County deed book A, p. 45, in Gleason McCubbin, p. 44.
296. Irene B. Webster, compiler, Rockingham County, North Carolina Will Abstracts, v. I, 1785-1865, p. 17. Also, Rockingham County deed book A, p. 84, in Patterson, 1988, p. 149.
297. Rouse, The Great Wagon Road, p. 116-117.
298. Clement, The History of Pittsylvania County, Virginia, p. 89.
299. Clement, The History of Pittsylvania County, Virginia, p. 91
300. McCubbin, "Nicholas Blind Nick McCubbin, 1780-1855."
301. Tucker, 1919, p. 18.
302. Patterson, Kennard, King, Knight, Hardin, Goodin, p.161-162.
303. Jordon Dodd, Kentucky Marriages, 1802-1850, Provo, UT, photocopy of

marriage fecord, https://www.ancestry.com,1997.
304. Patterson, Kennard, King, Knight, Hardin, Goodin, p. 181.
305. Patterson, Kennard, King, Knight, Hardin, Goodin, p. 170, 174, 185.
306. James P. McCubbin, Sr., https://www.findagrave.com, Vance Cemetery, Eve (unincorporated community), Green County, KY, memorial 100886139, CatheaC. No grave marker found, but it is likely that he is buried here. Information has been contributed by Carolyn McCubbins Scott and others, and photos of the Vance Cemetery were provided by CatheaC.
307. Patterson, Kennard, King, Knight, Hardin, Goodin, p. 145.
308. J. C. McCubbin, family information from letters, etc. in Patterson, 1988, p. 136
309. Green County, Kentucky, deed book 11, p. 90-91, in Patterson, 1988, p. 140-141.
310. J. C. McCubbin, family information in Patterson, 1988, p. 136.
311. Green County, Kentucky, wills, bk 2, p. 104, in Patterson, 1988, p. 146, 160.
312. James P. McCubbin, Sr., https://www.findagrave.com, Vance Cemetery, Eve, Green County, Missouri. No grave marker was found for James P. McCubbin, Sr.
313. National DAR #429341, in Patterson, 1988, p. 145-146.
314. Patterson, Kennard, King, Knight, Hardin, Goodin, p. 182-183.
315. 1850 U. S. Census, Green County, KY.
316. Patterson, Kennard, King, Knight, Hardin, Goodin, p. 136.
317. Green County, Kentucky, Court, in Patterson, 1988, p.146-147.
318. Patterson, Kennard, King, Knight, Hardin, Goodin, p. 145.
319. Robert E. McCubbin, personal communication, 1983, 1998. Also, https://www.findagrave.com, Vance\McCubbin Cemetery Green County, Kentucky; burials here include Zachariah (memorial 104837611), Nicholas (100805875), and Nicholas's wife, Matiltda Gumm (100806027).
320. https://www.glorecords.blm.gov, land patents, Hancock County, ILL.
321. White, Kelley, and Miles, 1969, v. 1, 38c-39; also, Patterson, 1988, p. 164-165.
322. John C. McCubbin, "Hancock County, ILL Pioneers," in Patterson, 1988, p.165.
323. John C. McCubbin, "Hancock County, ILL Pioneers," in Patterson, 1988, p. 164-165.
324. John C. McCubbin, "The Levi and Barbara Bloyd Letter," in Patterson, 1988, p. 166. Letter transcribed by John C. McCubbin.
325. John C. McCubbin, "The Levi and Barbara Bloyd Letter," in Patterson, 1988, p. 166.
326. John C. McCubbin, "Hancock County, ILL Pioneers," \in Patterson, 1988, p. 165. The Oak Grove Cemetery is shown on modern maps of the area.
327. John C. McCubbin, 'Hancock County, ILL Pioneers," in Patterson, 1988, p.167-168.
328. John C. McCubbin, in Levi Bloyd family tree, https://www.ancestry.com.
329. Patterson, Kennard, King, Knight, Hardin, Goodin, p. 165.
330. John C. McCubbin, "Hancock County, ILL Pioneers," in Patterson, 1988, p. 165.
331. Patterson, Kennard, King, Knight, Hardin, Goodin, p. 167.
332. John C. McCubbin, "Hancock County, ILL Pioneers," in Patterson, 1988, p. 166.
333. https://www.glorecords.blm.gov, Hancock County, ILL. Thomas Bloyd land patent, IL4060.401.
334. John C. McCubbin, "Hancock County, ILL Pioneers," in Patterson, 1988, p. 167.
335. John C. McCubbin, "Hancock County, ILL Pioneers," in Patterson, 1988, p.167.
336. John C. McCubbin, "Hancock County, ILL Pioneers," in Patterson, 1988, p. 167.

337. John C. McCubbin, "Hancock County, ILL Pioneers," in Patterson, 1988, p. 167.
338. Patterson, Kennard, King, Knight, Hardin, Goodin, p. 167.
339. Patterson, Kennard, King, Knight, Hardin, Goodin, p. 62-63; also, Bloyd family tree in https://www.ancestry.com.
340. John C. McCubbin (edited by Kenneth Zech), The McCubbin Papers, an Account of the Early History of Reedley and the "76 Country, Reedley Historical Society, Reedley CA, 1988.
341. Clyde Lee Jenkins, Judge Jenkins' History of Miller County, Missouri, Vol.1, Through the Civil War, 1971, reprinted 1995, p. 17.
342. Jenkins, Judge Jenkins' History of Miller County, Missouri, Vol. 1, p. 20.
343. Lake of the Ozarks State Park website, https://www.mostateparks.com/park/lake-ozarks- state-park.
344. Jenkins, Judge Jenkins' History of Miller County, Missouri, Vol.1, p 19.
345. Jenkins, Judge Jenkins' History of Miller County, Missouri, Vol.1, p. 88.
346. Jenkins, Judge Jenkins' History of Miller County, Missouri, Vol. 1, p. 17-18.
347. James Hunter Chapter of the National DAR, 1981, p. 34-35; Thomas P. DeGraffenreid, The DeGraffenreid Family Scrap Book, 1181-1957, Seven Hundred and Sixty-Five Years, (The University of Virginia Press, Charlottesville VA, 1958), p. 189.
348. Jenkins, Judge Jenkins' History of Miller County, Missouri, Vol. 1, p. 135.
349. Jenkins, Judge Jenkins' History of Miller County, Missouri, Vol. 1, p. 37.
350. Jenkins, Judge Jenkins' History of Miller County, Missouri, Vol. 1, p. 24-25.
351. Jenkins, Judge Jenkins' History of Miller County, Missouri, Vol. 1, p. 59-60.
352. Early Pioneer Writes Home, in Dedication of the Miller County Museum, June 14, 1980. A letter written in June, 1859, describes the farms In Miller County.
353. Kate McCubbin, in Kathlene Kelly White and Kathlene White Miles, The History of Benton County, Missouri, Vol. 1, (published by White & Miles, Clinton/Warsaw MO, 1969), p. 50j.
354. Patterson, Kennard, King, Knight, Hardin, Goodin, p. 160-161.
355. Kate McCubbin, in White and Miles, The History of Benton County, Missouri, Vol. 1, p. 50j-52j.
356. White and Miles, The History of Benton County, Missouri, Vol. 1. Map on p. 507 shows home of David McCubbin.
357. White and Miles, The History of Benton County, Missouri, Vol. 1. Photo of David's house.
358. Patterson, Kennard, King, Knight, Hardin, Goodin, p.161.
359. Burials of David and Amelia (Ella) McCubbin, Kinkaid Cemetery, near Warsaw, Benton Co., MO, https://www.findagrave.com. Memorials for David (21426928) and Ella (21426856) maintained by Linda Dukes.
360. Patterson, Kennard, King, Knight, Hardin, Goodin, p. 156; also, White and Miles, The History of Benton County Missouri, Vol. 1, p. 38c-39c.
361. Mrs. Clyde McCubbin, in Patterson, Kennard, King, Knight, Hardin, Goodin, p. 156; also, White and Miles, The History of Benton County Missouri, Vol. 1, p. 38c-39c.
362. Clyde Lee Jenkins, Family History in Miller County Dates from 1830s, Eldon County Missouri Advertiser, March 9, 1972. Newspaper Library, State Historical Society of Missouri, Columbus, LDS film 0908040. Submitted to Family History Library by Janet Roberts, microfilm 0982168.

363. Patterson, Kennard, King, Knight, Hardin, Goodin, p. 158.
364. Pleasant McCubbin burial in Kincaid Cemetery, Warsaw, Benton County, MO. https://www.findagrave.com, memorial 140858396 maintained by Linda Dukes.
365. John C McCubbin, in Patterson, 1988, p.167-168.
366. William H. Rupe household, 1850 U. S. Census, Benton County, MO; transcribed in Patterson, 1988, p. 181.
367. William H. and Eleanor Rupe burials, Lewis Roth Cemetery, Warrensburg, Johnson County, MO, https://www.findagrave.com, memorial for William (99322840) and Eleanor (135795269) maintained by Linda Dukes.
368. Patterson, Kennard, King, Knight, Hardin, Goodin, p. 168.
369. Walker, Karen (ed.), Major Molly Chapter of the D.A.R., USGenWeb Archives,1985.
370. Jenkins, Eldon Missouri Advertiser, March 9, 1972.
371. Jenkins, Eldon Missouri Advertiser, March 9, 1972.
372. Jenkins, Eldon Missouri Advertiser, March 9, 1972.
373. Jenkins, Judge Jenkins' History of Miller County, Missouri, Vol 1, p. 25-26.
374. https://www.glorecordsblm.org, Land Patents, Glaize Township, Miller County, MO. Land patents by John McCubbin and family.
375. Jenkins, Judge Jenkins' History of Miller County, Missouri, Vol.1, p. 53-54.
376. Jenkins, Judge Jenkins' History of Miller County, Missouri, Vol. 1, p. 65.
377. Jenkins, Judge Jenkins' History of Miller County, Missouri, Vol. 1, p..76-77.
378. https://www.glorecords.blm.gov, Land Patents, Glaize Township, Miller County, MO. Tscharner DeGraffenreid family.
379. Jenkins, Judge Jenkins' History of Miller County, Missouri, Vol. 1, p. 137.
380. Jenkins, Judge Jenkins' History of Miller County, Missouri, Vol. 1, p. 137.
381. Churches of Miller County, Brumley Baptist Church, Miller County Museum & Historical Society, p. 4-5, https://www.millercountymuseum.org.
382. Jenkins, Judge Jenkins' History of Miller County, Missouri, Vol. 1, p. 127-131.
383. John and Elizabeth McCubbin tombstones in the Hawkins Cemetery, near Brumley, Miller County, MO, https://www.findagrave.com. Memorials 1334444452 for John and 134444549 are maintained by Gone Too Soon.
384. Jenkins, Eldon Missouri Advertiser, March 9, 1972.
385. William R. and Nancy Bilyeu McCubbin are buried in the Logan Pleasant View Cemetery, Oregon City, Clackamus County, OR Cemetery, https://www.findagrave.com. Memorials for William R. (388138810) and Nancy (38813313) are maintained by JRC.
386. Town of Brumley, 50th Anniversary, Bagnell Dam, 1931-1981, (Miller County Historical Society, no date), p. 51-52.
387. Jenkins, Eldon Missouri Advertiser, March 9, 1972.
388. Jenkins, Judge Jenkins' History of Miller County, Missouri, Vol. 1, Miller County Marriages, book A, p. 143-172.
389. Jenkins, Eldon Missouri Advertiser, March 9, 1972.
390. Jenkins, Judge Jenkins' History of Miller County, Missouri, Vol. 1, p. 135.
391. Jenkins, Judge Jenkin's History of Miller County, Missouri, Vol. 1, p. 136.
392. Jenkins, Judge Jenkins' History of Miller County, Missouri, Vol. 1, p. 136; also, Churches of Miller County, https://www.millercountymuseum.org.
393. Jenkins, Judge Jenkins' History of Miller County, Missouri, Vol. 1, p. 136.19
394 Churches of Miller County, Hickory Point Baptist Church, https://www.

millercountymuseum.org, p. 11-12.
395. Jenkins, Eldon Missouri Advertiser, March 9, 1972.
396. James P. McCubbin, Jr. will, recorded October 22, 1841, Miller County Court; vol. A, pages 3-6, reel C11247, Missouri State Archives; also archived in DAR lineage application 1013432. A photocopy of the will was sent by Donald McCubbin on June 23, 2022 to the Miller County Museum in Tuscumbia, MO for their records.
397. Jenkins, Eldon Missouri Advertiser, March 9, 1972.
398. Jenkins, Judge Jenkins' History of Miller County, Missouri, Vol. 1, List of Miller County Marriages, Book A, p. 141-172.
399. https://www.glorecords.blm.gov, Land Patents, Richwood Township, Miller County, MO. James McCubbin family.
400. https://www.glorecords.blm.gov, Land Patents, Richwood Township, Miller County, MO.
401. Olive Waite Livingston. The Livingston Family of Miller County, [Missouri]. Miller County Homepage, https://www.rootsweb.com.
402. Tombstones for William C. McCubbin and wife, Margaret, https://www.findagrave.com, Livingston Cemetery, Iberia, Miller County, MO. Memorials for William C. (57067304) and Margaret (57067333) maintained by Nancy Thompson.
403. Jenkins, Judge Jenkins' History of Miller County, Missouri, Vol. 1, List of Marriages, p. 143-172. Zachariah and Susannah on p.148.
404. Jenkins, Judge Jenkins' History of Miller County, Missouri, Vol.1, p. 136.
405. Jenkins, Judge Jenkins' History of Miller County, Missouri, Vol. 1, p. 135; also, https://www.findagrave.com.
406. Jenkins, Judge Jenkins' History of Miller County, Missouri, Vol. 1, List of Marriages, p. 143-172.
407. Hugh Jenkins genealogy, personal correspondence; also, Olive Waite Livingstone, Miller County Homepage, https://www.rootsweb.com.
408. https://www.glorecords.blm.gov, Land Patents, Richwood Township, Miller County, Tscharner DeGraffenreid family.
409. Jenkins, Judge Jenkins' History of Miller County, Missouri, Vol. 1, 1995, List of Marriages, p. 143-172.
410. Wayne Sampson, compiler, Descendants of Bravester (Bannister) Barton. Personal correspondence to Donald McCubbin on December 12, 2005.
411. http://www.glorecords.blm.gov. Land Patents. Richwood Township, Miller County, Barton family.
412. Tombstones for Bentley and Elizabeth Barton and daughter Mary Frances and her husband James McCubbin, https://www.findagrave.com>, Hickory Point Cemetery, Iberia, Miller County, MO. Memorials for Bentley (5713171), Elizabeth (5713173), their daughter Mary Frances (134601705), and her husband James Albert McCubbin (5713204) were sourced by Wayne Sampson.
413. https://www.glorecords.blm.gov, Land Patents, Richwood Township, Miller County, Livingston family.
414. Jenkins, Judge Jenkins' History of Miller County, Missouri, Vol. 1, Miller County Marriages.
415. Tombstone for Mary E. (McCubbin) Livingston, https://www.findagrave.com, Livingston Cemetery, Iberia, Miller County MO.

416. Olive Waite Livingston, Miller County Homepage, https://www.rootsweb.com.
417. Jenkins, Judge Jenkins' History of Miller County, Missouri, Vol. 1, p. 223
418. https://www.glorecords.blm.gov. Land patents, Richwood Township, Miller County, William Watkins.
419. Robert L. Hays and Etta Jane Hays, Descendants of Toliver Jeffries and Mary "Polly" Warner Jeffries of Virginia, Kentucky, and Missouri, Vol. 1, 2003, p. 566. Self-published.
420. Jenkins, Judge Jenkins' History of Miller County, Missouri, Vol. 1, p. 223.
421. Peggy Hake Smith, 1991, pg. 57-58; also, https://www.findagrave.com, Hickory Point Cemetery, Iberia, Miller County, MO.
422. Jenkins, Judge Jenkins' History of Miller County, Missouri, Vol.1, p. 116-123.
423. Clyde Lee Jenkins, Judge Jenkins' History of Miller County, Missouri, Vol. 2, End of the Civil War through 1900, self-published, 1971, republished, 1997, p. 1.
424. Jenkins, Judge Jenkins' History of Miller County, Missouri, Vol. 1, p. 177.
425. Jenkins, Judge Jenkins' History of Miller County, Missouri, Vol. 1, p
426. Jenkins, Judge Jenkins' History of Miller County, Missouri, Vol. 1, p. 204.
427. Jenkins, Judge Jenkins' History of Miller County, Missouri, Vol. 1, p. 204.
428. Jenkins, Judge Jenkins' History of Miller County, Missouri, Vol. 1, p. 180-181.
429. Jenkins, Judge Jenkins' History of Miller County, Missouri, Vol. 1, p. 208-209.
430. Jenkins, Judge Jenkins' History of Miller County, Missouri, Vol. 1, p. 211-212.
431. Jenkins, Judge Jenkins' History of Miller County, Missouri, Vol. 1, p. 216.
432. Jenkins, Judge Jenkins' History of Miller County, Missouri, Vol. 1, p. 229.
433. Abraham McCubbin is identified on a monument as one of those killed in the Lone Jack Battle and is buried at the Lone Jack Cemetery, Jackson County, MO, https://www.findagrave.com, memorial 29479149.
434. William C. McCubbin, died in Rolla Missouri and is buried at Livingston Cemetery, Iberia, Miller County, MO, https://www.findagrave.com, memorial 57067304.
435. Jenkins, Judge Jenkins' History of Miller County, Missouri, Vol. 2, p. 1.
436. Jenkins, Judge Jenkins' History of Miller County, Missouri, Vol. 2, p. 4-5.
437. Jenkins, Judge Jenkins' History of Miller County, Missouri, Vol. 2, p. 4-5.
438. Minutes of the Churches of Miller County, https://www.millercountymuseum.org.
439. Hays, and Hays, Descendants of Toliver Jeffries and Mary "Polly" Warner Jeffries of Virginia, Kentucky, and Missouri, Vol. 1, p. 566.
440. Jenkins, Judge Jenkins' History of Miller County, Missouri, Vol. 2, p. 4-5.
441. Olive Waite Livingston, Miller County Homepage, https://www.rootsweb.com.
442. Keo0lly Waman Stallings, Watkins, Miller County Communities, https://www.millercountymuseum.org. 1904 plat of land ownership in Watkins community.
443. Kelly Warman Stallings, Watkins, Miller County Communities, http://www.millercountymuseum.org.
444. James Albert McCubbin, his wife Mary Francis McCubbin, and Silas B. McCubbin, and his three wives are buried at Hickory Point Cemetery, Iberia, Miller County, MO, https://www.findagrave.com, memorial.
445. Lewis McCubbin and Jemimah Barton marriage performed by Jacob S. McComb, Elder, record no. 469, Miller County Clerk and Recorder, filed August 6th, 1868. Also, Wayne Sampson, 2005, family genealogy data, pers. comm, December 12, 2005.

446. Lake of the Ozarks State Park website, https://www.lakeoftheOzarksstatepark.
447. Jeffries and Huddleston families, https://www.glorecords.blm.gov.
448. DeGraffenreid family, https://www.glorecords.blm.gov.
449. Birth records, Camden County, on https://www.ancestry.com.
450. Lewis McCubbin, https://www.glorecords.blm.gov, Land Patents, Camden County.
451. 50th Anniversary, Bagnell Dam, 1931-1981, p. 30, (Miller County Historical Society). Zebra was on a ridge about one-half mile west of present highway 54 on what would become lake road 54-30.
452. Foxen and Blankenship family patents, https://www.glorecords.blm.gov, Land Patents, Miller and Camden Counties, MO.
453. Degraffenreid family patents, https://www.glorecords.blm.gov, land patents, Camden Counties, MO.
454. Donald McCubbin, personal observation and photos on visit in October, 1995.
455. General warranty deed, signed by both L. C. and Jemimah McCubbin, February 2, 1894, Camden County, MO, land records, DB 51, p. 252.
456. Indenture signed by L. C. McCubbin, recorded November 25, 1919, by Aubrey Shipman, Camden County, DB 37, p. 435; also, Robert L. Hays, and Etta Jane Hays, Descendants of Toliver Jeffries and Mary "Polly" Warner Jeffries of Virginia, Kentucky, and Missouri, Volume 1, 2003, p. 654, (self-published, Golden CO).
457. Missouri Department of Natural Resources, land records, DB 85, 195.
458. Etta Jane Hays, letter to Donald McCubbin and other family members, Oct. 24, 2005. Photos of the roadside marker and a list of those buried at Auglaize Cemetery was provided by that letter, and photos of some of the surviving gravestones in the cemetery are included in the memorials on http//www.findagrave.org.
459. Hays, Robert L. and Hays, Etta Jane, 2003, p. 654; Thomas P. DeGraffenreid, The DeGraffenreid Family Scrapbook,1181-1957, Seven Hundred and Sixty-Five Years, (The University of Virginia Press, Charllottesville VA, 1958).
460. Sharon A. Shipman,1988, reprinted 1996, p.39-42. Also, Memorial to Judge James D. Shipman, September 1, 1897, unknown newspaper, in files of Donald McCubbin.
461. C. B. Shipman obituary. Lake Sun Leader. November 8, 1986.
462. Clara Snapp, pers. comm. to Donald McCubbin. Rock wall also observed by Donald McCubbin.
463. Henryetta, Oklahoma, City Directory, 1917 and 1922, Dunhan Directory Company, Springfield MO.
464. Ella Nora McCubbin obituary. "Funeral Rites for Ella McCubbin." Henryetta Free Lance, July 2, 1961. Also, https://www.findagrave.com, West Lawn Cemetery, Henryetta, Okmulgee County, OK, memorial 142369837.
465. Zachariah (Z. M.) McCubbin obituary. "Long-time Resident Succumbs in Ohio." Henryetta Free Press, March 6, 1963. Tombstone at Valley View Memorial Gardens, Xenia, Greene County, OH, https://www.findagrave.com.
466. C. B. McCubbin and Bernice Ray Wilson marriage license. Camden County recorder of deeds, book 1, page 381, certified copy, 6 December 1951. Also, Certificate of Marriage, July 12,1908, signed by Jno. W. Jeffries, M. G.
467. Fred Wilson obituary, Perkins [Oklahoma] Journal, date unknown. From Pauline

McCubbin Holbrook, forwarded to Donald McCubbin by Linda Holbrook.
468. Birth records, children of C. B. and Bernice McCubbin, Camden County, MO.
469. Doyle Wayne McCubbin tombstone, Glencoe, Payne County, Oklahoma Cemetery, https://www.findagrave.com, memorial 276942493.
470. James Oliver McCubbin obituary, unidentified newspaper, files of Donald McCubbin.
471. Alta Jeffries McCubbin obituary, unidentified newspaper, files of Donald McCubbin.
472. James Oliver McCubbin and wife Alta Pearl Jeffries tombstones, near Kaiser, New Hope Cemetery, MO, https://www.findagrave.com, memorials for James Oliver (5710846) and Alta (5710859) contributed by Wayne Sampson.
473. Robert K. and Pernicia McCubbin Jeffries tombstones, Jeffries Family Cemetery, Miller County, MO, https://www.findagrave.com, memorials for Robert (5706436) and Pernicia (5706606) by Wayne Sampson.
474. Suellen McCubbin White, letter May 3, 2004 to Donald McCubbin. Suellen, the granddaughter of Merrill "Mac" McCubbin, writes that the birth dates for Merrill and Carroll are from the family bible kept by Merrill's wife Leticia.
475. Photo by Addie Wallis Moulder in about 1920-1921 and included in her book "Journey Though Passover." It was later verified by both Addie and Alice Burns that the photo was made at McCubbins Ford, where it crosses Auglaize Creek; photo provided to Donald McCubbin by Clara Snapp.
476. Suellen McCubbin White, letter May 3, 2004 to Donald McCubbin.
477. Newspaper clippings from The Reveille, Linn Creek, Missouri newspaper, in files of Donald McCubbin.
478. Suellen McCubbin White, letter May 3, 2004 to Donald McCubbin.
479. Passover school records for 1883, 1893, 1894, and 1899; transcribed by Clara Snapp. Copies in files of Donald McCubbin.
480. Photos provided by Clara Snapp, pers. comm. to Donald Mc Cubbin.
481. Passover, 50th Anniversary, Bagnell Dam, 1931-1981, Miller County Historical Society, p. 24-26, special publication.
482. Passover, 50th Anniversary, Bagnell Dam, 1931-1981, Miller County Historical Society, p. 24-26, special publication.
483. J. W. Vincent, compiler, "Camden County History," https://www.rootsweb.com.
484. J. W. Vincent, compiler, "Camden County History," https://www.rootsweb.com.
485. Etta Jane Hays, letter to Donald McCubbin, October 24, 2005; also, https://www,findagrave.com, Auglaize Cemetery Camden County, MO.
486. Camden County property records, DB 51, p. 333, Camden County, MO.
487. Camden County property records, DB 67, p.196, Camden County, MO.
488. Camden County property records, DB 85, p. 195, Camden County, MO.
489. 50th Anniversary, Bagnell Dam,1931-1981, Miller County Historical Society.
490. Photo from Clara Snapp, personal communication to Donald McCubbin. Also, memorial to James D. Shipman, September 1, 1897, unknown newspaper, copy in files of Donald McCubbin.
491. Lewis C. McCubbin death certificate no. 19086, Missouri State Board of Health. Obituary in Eldon Advertiser, June 9, 1933. Also, tombstones at Freedom Church of Christ Cemetery, Linn Creek, Camden County MO, https://www.findagrave.com, memorial 39673203. The death certificate shows the name spelled "Louis", but other records show "Lewis."

492. Ray McCubbin, Freedom Church of Christ Cemetery, Linn Creek, Camden County MO, https://www.findagrave.com, memorial 39673063.
493. Jemimah McCubbin obituary, unidentified newspaper, 1944. Also, Freedom Cemetery, Linn Creek, MO, https://www.findagrave.com, memorial 39673501.
494. Photo by Addie Wallis Moulder, collected by Clara Snapp, personal comm. to Donald McCubbin.
495. Newspaper photo of Passover students, from Clara Snapp.
496. Suellen McCubbin White, pers. comm., letter to Donald McCubbin, May 3, 2004.
497. Merrill "Mac" McCubbin, Wild Food & Other Outdoor Drivel, self-published, copy in files of Donald McCubbin.
498. Letter from Merrill McCubbin to local resident, Alice Burns, written by Merrill in January, 1975; copy provided to this author by Clara Snapp is in the files of Donald McCubbin.
499. Tombstone for Merrill (Mac) McCubbin, Freedom Church of Christ Cemetery, Linn Creek, Camden County, MO, https://www.findagrave.com, memorial 39742916.
500. Robert E. Cunningham, Stillwater, Where Oklahoma Began, (Arts and Humanities Council of Stillwater, Oklahoma, Colorgraphics, Oklahoma City, OK, 1969), p. viii.
501. Cunningham, Stillwater, Where Oklahoma Began, p. viii.
502. Pauline McCubbin Holbrook, pers. comm. to Donald McCubbin.
503. Pauline McCubbin Holbrook, pers. comm. to Donald McCubbin.
504. https://www.glolandrecords.gov.
505 Pauline McCubbin Holbrook, pers. comm. to Donald McCubbin.
506. Doyle Wayne McCubbin, pers comm. to Donald McCubbin.
507. Pauline McCubbin Holbrook, pers. comm. to Donald McCubbin.
508. Lincoln County Historical Society, History of Lincoln County, (Country Press, Chandler, OK, 1988), p. 252.
509. Lincoln County Historical Society, History of Lincoln County, (Country Press, Chandler, OK, 1988), p. 252.
510. Pauline McCubbin Holbrook, pers. comm. to Donald McCubbin.
511. Earl D. Newsom, The Story of Exciting Payne County, (New Forums Press, 1997), p. 150, 157.
512. Glenn McCubbin, pers comm. to Donald McCubbin.
513. Edman Gale McCubbin, pers. communication to Donald McCubbin.
514. Donald McCubbin, pers. observation.
515. Grave marker for Doyle Wayne McCubbin, https://www.findagrave.com, memorial 27657135, maintained by Marietta McCubbin.
516. Donald McCubbin, pers. observation.
517. Carl Bruell McCubbin death certificate no. 016493, Oklahoma Department of Health; also, Obituary, Carl Bruell McCubbin, Stillwater News Press. Grave marker for Carl Bruell McCubbin, Glencoe Cemetery, Payne County, Oklahoma; https://www.findagrave.com, memorial 27657135, maintained by Marietta McCubbin.
518. Bernice Ray McCubbin death certificate (number illegible on certified copy), Missouri Division of Health, Jefferson, MO. Also, Obituary, Stillwater News Press, January 11, 1965.

519. Grave marker for Bernice McCubbin, Glencoe Cemetery, Payne County, OK, https://www.findagrave.com, memorial 27657177, maintained by Marietta McCubbin.

Selected Bibliography

Abercrummie, William, A Description of Carrict, The Geographical Collections Relating to Scotland Collected by Waltr MacFarlane of the Ilk, Esquire, and Reprinted Subsequently, as "Carrick in 1696," with comments by Dave Killicoat, December 2002, Maybole, Ayrshire, from website, https://www.maybole.org/history/books/abercrummie/carrick1696.

Alsop, George, A Character of the Province of Maryland, 1666, Facsimile reproduction, with Introduction by Robert A. Bain, (York Mail Print, Inc. Bainbridge, NY, 1972.)

[American Revolution troops], Muster Rolls and Other Records of Service of Maryland Troops in the American Revolution, 1775-1783, (Baltimore Maryland Historical Society, Lord Baltimore Press, Baltimore, 1900); Archives of Maryland, Hall of Records Library, 350 Rowe Blvd, Annapolis Maryland Historical Society, 1900.

Anderson, Elizabeth B., Annapolis: A Walk Through History, (Tidewater Publishers, Centreville MD, 1984), Maryland State Archives, microfilm CR37,501.

Anderson, Patricia Abelard, Frederick County Maryland Land Records: Liber E (Printprint Archives, July 1995), Maryland State Archives, microfilm C 37,501

Ayrshire Archaeological and Natural History Society, The Carrick Covenant of 1638, https://www.aanhsorg.files.wordpress.com 2018/08 PDF, p. 107-118.

Baldwin, Jane (ed.), The Maryland Calendar of Wills, Vols. II and III. (Kohn & Pollock, Publishers, Baltimore MD, 1906; reprinted by Genealogical Publishing Co., 1968). Abstract of wills of John Maccubin and Samuel Howard.

Barnes, Robert, Maryland Marriages, 1634-1777, (Genealogical Publishing Co., Baltimore MD, 1975).

Barnes, Robert William, Colonial Families of Anne Arundel County, Maryland, (Family Line Publications, Westminster MD, 1995).

Beatty, Edith Worley, The Waters Book; Genealogy of Waters and Allied Families, Posthumous Papers, Maryland Historical Society, item 34, n.p.1956?

Black, George F., The Surnames of Scotland: Their Origin, Meaning, and History, (Birlinn Limited, Edinburgh, 1946).

[Brampton house]. "Old McCubbin House at Brampton," nomination Form for the National Register of Historic Places and Architectural Survey File AA-161, last updated 6-11-2004, National Park Service. Copied from records of Donna M. Ware, Annapolis MD for Donald McCubbin, June, 2001.

[Brampton ownership]. Outline of ownership of Brampton based on wills, deeds, mortgages, etc.: prepared for the Anne Arundel Office of Law, files of the Department of Planning and Code Enforcement, Anne Arundel County. Copied from records of Donna M. Ware, Historic Sites Planner, for Donald McCubbin in June 2002.

Browne, William Hand, ed., Archives of Maryland. Journal of the Maryland

Convention, July 26 - August 14, 1775, Journal and Correspondence of the Maryland Council of Safety, August 29, 1775 - July 6, 1776, Maryland Historical Society, 1892.

Carr, Lois Green, and Menard, Russell R., Immigration and Opportunity: The Freedman in Early Colonial Maryland, in The Chesapeake in the Seventeenth Century, (Thad W. Tate and David L. Ammerman, eds., New York, 1979).

Carroll, Douglas, Jr., "Families of Dr. Charles Carroll (1691-1755) and Cornet Thomas Dewey (160x-1648)," unpublished manuscript. Contains wills of Charles Carroll, the Barrister, and Nicholas Maccubbin.

Carter, Robert W., Jr., "A History of Wolf Island Primitive Baptist Church." Journal of Rockingham County History and Genealogy, vol. IX, no. 1, June, 1984, p. 1-17.

Clement, Maud Carter, The History of Pittsylvania County, Virginia, (J. P. Hill Company, Lynchburg VA, 1929).

Cunningham, Robert E., Stillwater Where Oklahoma Began, (Arts and Humanities Council of Stillwater, ColorGraphics, Oklahoma City OK, 1969).

DAR Patriot Index, Centennial Ed., Part II, (Daughters of the American Revolution, National Society, Washington, 1990). Cites James, Nicholas, and Richard McCubbin/McCubin.

Davidson, Walter Craig, Family Research: Davidson/McNabb/McNeil/Buckner/Cloud/Taylor/McCubbin/Lane or Layne and Kuykindall, Record Management/Micrographics, Salt Lake City, 1966, microfilm, 1 reel; Library of Virginia.

Dean, Jane, Extracts from Jane Dean's writings, approximately early 1900s.Typescript provided by Michael and Robyn Oliver, 164 Main North Road, RD 21, Geraldine, New Zealand, to Douglas Calderwood, Knockdolian Estate, personal communication to Donald McCubbin, October 19, 2005.

Dobson, David, Scots on the Chesapeake,1621-1776, revised edition, (Genealogical Publishing Company, Baltimore MD, 2012).

Dorsey, Caleb, "Original Land Grants of the South Side of Severn River," Maryland Historical Magazine, vol. 53, no. 4 (December, 1958), p. 394-400. Map and list of early land grants and their original owners, including John Maccubbin.

Drynan, David and T. Kennedy, "History of Knockdolian, VII, p. 52-53, and VIII, p. 70-71." Scottish Notes and Queries, Vol. VI, 3rd series, March, 1928.

Drynan, David and T. Kennedy, "History of Knockdolian, IX, p. 90-91." Scottish Notes and Queries, Vol. VI, 3rd series, May, 1928.

Earle, Carville V., The Evolution of a Tidewater Settlement System: All Hallow's Parish, Maryland, 1650-1783, (The University of Chicago Department of Geography Research Paper No. 170, Chicago ILL, 1975).

Fergusson, Sir James, By the Water of Girvan, People and Places in South Ayrshire History, (The Grimsay Press, Glasgow, 2005).

Gary, Joy, "Patrick Craig of Annapolis," Maryland Historical Magazine, vol. 48, no. 4, December, 1953, p. 310-326.

Hake, Peggy Smith, Pioneer Families of Miller County, Missouri: Journey to the Past, (privately published).

Hays, Robert L., and Hays, Etta Jane, Descendants of Toliver Jeffries and Mary "Polly" Warner Jeffries of Virginia, Kentucky, and Missouri, Volume 1, 2003, (privately published, Robert L. Hays, 322 Lookout Ct., Golden CO 2003).

Imbrie, John D., The Carrick Covenant of 1638, Publications online, Archeological and Natural History Society, website https://www.aanhsorg.files.wordpress.

com>2018/08PDF, p. 107-118.

[Java, Squirrel Neck plantation], "Java, Contee House (ruin)," Inventory Form for State Historic Sites Survey, Maryland Historical Trust. Copied from records of Donna M. Ware.

Jenkins, Clyde Lee, Judge Jenkins' History of Miller County, Missouri, Vol 1, Through the Civil War, (published by the author, Tuscumbia MO, 1971. Republished by Clayton Edwin Jenkins, 1995).

Jenkins, Clyde Lee, Judge Jenkins' History of Miller County, Missouri, Vol. 2, End of Civil War through 1900, (published by the author, Tuscumbia Missouri, 1971; republished by Clayton Edwin Jenkins, Tuscumbia MO, 1997).

Jenkins, Clyde Lee, "Family History in Miller County Dates from 1830s," Eldon [Missouri] Advertiser, March 9, 1972; newspaper library, State Historical Society of Missouri, Columbus, LDS film 0908040; submitted to Family History Library by Janet Roberts, microfilm 0982168.

Jenkins, Hugh, 4304 Bridgeboro Rd., Moorestown, NJ, 08057-3732. Family history data base or tree, gedcom file, received from Jenkins in February 2000 and loaded into personal FYM file, McCubbin1 database: uploaded with some additions by Donald McCubbin to https://www.familytreemaker.com.

Keck, Kim, "Friends, Tobacco, and Slavery: First Patuxent Meeting, 1666-1817," manuscript, 2003, in Patuxent Friends (Quaker) Meeting website, https://www.patentfriends.org.

Kelly, J. Reaney, Quakers in the Founding of Anne Arundel County, Maryland, (Maryland Historical Society, Baltimore MD, 1963).

Lincoln County Historical Society, Lincoln County [Oklahoma] History, (Country Lane Press, Chandler, Oklahoma, 1988).

Lindauer, Anthony D., From Paths to Plats, the Development of Annapolis, 1651-1718, (The Maryland State Archives and The Maryland Historical Trust, 1997).

Livingston, Olive Waite, The Livingston Family of Miller County [Missouri], undated, http://www.rootsweb.com/momiller/Livingston. Recollections about the Livingston and Castleman families, 1813-1966.

Loeser, Rudolf, "John Maccubbin of Anne Arundel County and His Children," Maryland Genealogical Society Bulletin, vol. 40, no. 2 (Spring, 1999), p. 159-245.

MacKenzie, George Norbury (ed.), Colonial Families of the United States of America, vol. IV, (Genealogical Publishing Co., Baltimore MD, 1966).

Magruder, P. H., "A Walk Through Annapolis in Bygone Days." U. S. Naval Institute Proceedings, Annapolis Maryland, 1931. Includes a reproduction of a painting "Washington Opens Ball with Mrs. James Mackubin".

Martin, Sheila L., "Knockdolian, the Seat of the McKubbens: Sir John McCubbin of Knockdolian and His Descendants in Anne Arundel County, Maryland," Maryland Genealogical Society Bulletin, vol. 25, no. 3 (Summer 1984), p. 287-293.

[M'Connel, William], "The Late Mr. William M'Connell of Knockdolian," article from unknown newspaper dated October 23, 1902, provided to Donald McCubbin on October 28, 2002 by Douglas Calderwood, Knockdolian Estate, Colmonell/Girvan, Ayrshire, Scotland.

McCubbin, Donald, Genealogical "tree" or database, McCubbin and associated families, based on family tree compiled by Hugh Jenkins, gedcom file, downloaded to Donald McCubbin familytreemaker.com file. This file, which includes added information on more recent generations was uploaded to https://www.ancestry.com for more general access.

McCubbin family history website, https://www.mccubbinfamily.info. Includes results and analysis of McCubbin DNA from website familytreedna.com; also includes records of the early McCubbins (mostly in Latin or Old Scots) transcribed by Edinburgh researcher Diane Baptie, compiled by Lorna McCubbin, and archived under the sections "Knockdolian" and "Miscellany."

McCubbin, Gleason Moss, "Nicholas 'Blind Nick' McCubbin, 1780-1855: His Ancestors and His Descendants, 1980," unpublished manuscript, Green County Public Library, Greensburg KY.

McCubbin, Gleason Moss, John P. Little (McCubbin): His Ancestors and His Descendants, self-published, Family History Library, Salt Lake City UT; fiche no. 11755, May 1, 1999.

McCubbin, John C., "The History of Hancock Township, Hancock County, Illinois," attached to Bloyd family tree in https://www.ancestry.com.tree/2034867i; also in Patterson, 1988, p. 164-166, in condensed form.

McCubbin, John C. (ed. by Kenneth Zech), "The McCubbin Papers, an Early History of Reedley and the '76 Country," Reedley Historical Society, Reedley, CA, 1988. The autobiography of the author, John C. McCubbin, is on p.193-209.

[McCubbin, Pauline Holbrook], "This Homemaker is Board of Education Secretary," Perkins [Oklahoma] Journal, date unknown, but probably June 15. 1981. Newspaper article based on an interview with Pauline Holbrook.

McCubbin, Robert E. Cemeteries of Green County, Kentucky, vol. 3, 1983. Transcribed to USGenWeb, archives for Green Co., KY in 1998.

McCubbin, Robert E., "Descendants of Kenneth Aplin I." Genealogy report printed from Family Tree Maker file, and sent to Donald McCubbin, June 1999. This file was evidently based on the gedcom file of Hugh Jenkins, perhaps with material added by Robert McCubbin.

McIntire, Robert Harry, Annapolis Maryland Families, (Gateway Press, Baltimore MD, 1979).

McWilliams, Jane W., "Howard's Inheritance, AA0136," Historical research and documentation, Annapolis MD, May 1996.

Mehrniger, Mrs. E., McCubbin Family Papers, self-published, Chicago IL, probably 1965. Genealogical Society of the Church of Jesus Christ of Latter-Day Saints, microfilmed June 10, 1983, item 5, XL1B7p102.

Menard, Russell R., Immigrants and Their Increase, in Law, Society, and Politics in Early Maryland, Aubrey C. Land, Lois Green Carr, and Edward C. Papenfuse, eds., Baltimore MD, 1977.

Meyer, Mary Keysor, Divorces and Names Changed in Maryland, by Act of the Legislature, 1634-1854. Laws changing names of James and Nicholas Jr. McCubbin.

[Miller County history], Dedication, Miller County Museum, June 14, 1980, (Miller County Historical Society, Tuscumbia, Missouri, 1980. Many short articles, newspaper format.

[Miller County history], 50th Anniversary, Bagnell Dam, 1931-1981, Miller County Historical Society, 1981-1981. Many short articles, newspaper format.

[Miller County history], Miller County Historical Society, June 17, 1983. Many short articles, newspaper format.

Moffat, Alistair, The Scots, A Genetic Journey, (Birlinn Limited, Edinburgh, 2017).

Muster Rolls and Records of Maryland, 1775-1783, Archives of Maryland, Maryland Historical Society, 1900.

Newman, Harry Wright, Anne Arundel Gentry. vol. 2, (published by the author, Annapolis MD, 1971).

Newman, Harry Wright, Anne Arundel Gentry, a Genealogical History of Some Early Families of Anne Arundel County, Maryland, vol. 3, (self-published, Annapolis MD, 1979).

Newsom, D. Earl, The Story of Exciting Payne County, (New Forums Press, Stillwater OK, 1997). "Danced with Washington: Mrs. James McCubbin of Annapolis Enjoyed That Honor," New York Times, May 19, 1895. This newspaper article also includes a portrait of Mrs. James Maccubbin.

Paterson, James, History of the Counties of Ayr & Wigton (Scotland). Volume II: Carrick. (James Stille, Edinburgh, 1864).

Patterson, Alta Kennard, edited by Virginia Fern Mitchell, Kennard, King, Knight, Hardin, Goodin: Their Ancestors & Descendants, (genealogical report, self-published, and printed by BookCrafters, 140 Buchanan St., Chelsea Michigan 48118, 1988).

[Pauline McCubbin Holbrook], "This Homemaker is Board of Education Secretary," Perkins [Oklahoma] Journal, date unknown.

Payne, Clyde William, The Brigs of Ayr: The Ancestry of MacCubbin (Gateway Press, Inc., Baltimore MD, 1999).

[Revolutionary war], Early Families of the North Carolina Counties of Rockingham and Stokes, with Revolutionary Service., compiled by James Hunter Chapter, Daughters of the American Revolution, of Madison, North Carolina, 1977. James (p. 80-81, John (p. 81-81), Nicholas McCubbin, (p. 27, 81-82).

Revolutionary War Pension and Bounty Land Warrant Application Files, 1800-1900, records of the Department of Veterans Affairs, Record Group 15, National Archives. Includes record for James McCubbin.

Ridgely, Helen W., Historic Graves of Maryland and the District of Columbia, (Genealogical Publishing Company, Baltimore, 1967; originally published by The Grafton Press, New York, 1908).

Ridout, Orland V., photograph of "Contee, View from West, February, 1971," AA-146. From the records of Donna M. Ware, Anne Arundel County, Maryland.

Riley, Elihu S., The Ancient City: History of Annapolis, in Maryland, 1649-1887, (Clearfield Company, Genealogical Publishing Co., Baltimore, Maryland,1995).

Risjord, Norman K., Builders of Annapolis: Enterprise and Politics in a Colonial Capital, (Maryland Historical Society, Baltimore Maryland, 1997).

Robertson, William, Ayrshire: Its History and Historic Families, Vol. 1, (Stephen & Pollack, Ayr, 1908. Reprinted by Forgotten books.com, London).

Rouse, Parke, Jr. The Great Wagon Road, (The Dietz Press, Richmond VA. Reprinted 2008).

Salter, Mike, The Castles of South-West Scotland, (Folly Publications, Malvern, Worc., 2006).

Sampson, Wayne, Descendants of Bavester (Bannister) Barton, genealogical report transmitted by letter to Donald McCubbin. December 12, 2005.

Shipman, Sharon A. Tabin, Worthy Names to Bear: Shipman, Blankenship, (published by the author, 1988; reprinted 1996).

Smith, Peggy Hake, Pioneer Families of Miller County, Missouri: Journey to the Past, copied from Bemis Library, Littleton Colorado.

Stein, Charles Francis, Jr., Origin and History of Howard County, Maryland, (Howard County Historical Society, Baltimore MD 1972).

Tranter, Nigel, The Fortified House in Scotland, vol. 5, North and West Scotland and Miscellaneous, (W. & R. Chambers Ltd. Edinburgh and London, 1970).

Trostel, Michael F., Mount Clare, Being an Account of the Seat Built by Charles Carroll, Barrister, upon His Lands at Patapsco, (The National Society of the Colonial Dames of America in the State of Maryland, Baltimore MD, acknowledgements May 1981).

Vincent, J. W., Camden County History, a compilation by the former editor of The Reveille of Linn Creek, Missouri, from interviews with early settlers, https://www.rootsweb.com, 11/14/2005.

Walker, Karen, and Williams, Marilyn, Historical Data Compiled by Major Molly Chapter, DAR, 1933-1934, retyped and indexed by Karen Walker, 1281 NW Bus. 36 Hwy, Hamilton MO, 1985, USGenWeb Archives. Includes article, McCubbin Family as Pioneers near Breckenridge, narrated by M. R. McCubbin, Breckenridge, 1995.

Ware, Donna M., Anne Arundel's Legacy: The Historic Properties of Anne Arundel County, (Environment and Special Project Division, Office of Planning and Zoning, Anne Arundel County, Annapolis MD, 1990).

Warfield, J. D., The Founders of Anne Arundel and Howard Counties, Maryland: A Genealogical and Biographical Review from Wills, Deeds and Church Records, (Kohn & Pollack, Publishers, Baltimore MD, 1905, reprinted by Regional Publishing Co., 1980).

Webster, Irene B., compiler, Rockingham County, North Carolina, Will Abstracts, v. 1, 1785-1865. (John Maccubbin will, probated May 1809, p. 84.)

[Wellesley], Arthur Valerian Wellesley, 8th Duke of Wellington, https://www.wikipedia.org/wiki/arthur/Valerian Wellesley,_8[th]_Duke[Wellesley], Lady Charlotte Anne Wellesley, https://www.thepeerage.com/.

Welsh, Luther W., Ancestral Colonial Families: Genealogy of the Welsh and Hyatt Families of Maryland and Their Kin, (Lambert Moon Printing Co., Independence MO, 1928).

White, Kathlene Kelly, and Miles, Kathlene White, The History of Benton County, Missouri, vol. l, (White & Miles, Clinton/Warsaw MO, 1969).

White, Suellen McCubbin, McCubbin Family Genealogy, Vol. 1, self-published, no date. Includes a genealogical history of the McCubbin family line from John Maccubbin of Maryland to James Merrill McCubbin, Jr. and his family,

Wright, Barbara, Green County, Kentucky, Will Records. Will Books I and II and Inventory Book II, (McDowell Publications, Utica KY, 1986).

Wright, F. Edward, Anne Arundel County Church Records of the 17th and 18th Centuries, (Family Line Publications, Westminster Maryland, no date).

Wright, Louis B., The Cultural Life of the American Colonies, 1607-1763, (Harper & Brothers, New York, 1957).

www.ingramcontent.com/pod-product-compliance
Lightning Source LLC
Chambersburg PA
CBHW040311240426
43666CB00022B/2928